CALEDON

CALEDON

NICOLA ROSS

WITH PHOTOGRAPHY BY GORD HANDLEY

The BOSTON
MILLS PRESS

To the Grahams of
Bishop's Mills.
I hope you'll enjoy
the book — especially
Thomas Graham's words.
N. Ross
Dec. 99

First published in 1999 *by*
BOSTON MILLS PRESS
132 Main Street, Erin, Ontario, N0B 1T0
Tel: 519-833-2407   Fax: 519-833-2195
e-mail: books@boston-mills.on.ca   www.boston-mills.on.ca

Distributed in Canada by
General Distribution Services Limited
325 Humber College Boulevard, Toronto, Canada M9W 7C3
Orders (Ontario & Quebec): 1-800-387-0141
Orders (NW Ontario & Other Provinces): 1-800-387-0172
e-mail: customer.service@ccmailgw.genpub.com
EDI Canadian Telebook: S1150391

An affiliate of
STODDART PUBLISHING CO. LIMITED
34 Lesmill Road, Toronto, Ontario, Canada M3B 2T6
Tel: 416-445-3333   Fax: 416-445-5967
e-mail: gdsinc@genpub.com   www.genpub.com

Distributed in the United States by
General Distribution Services Inc.
85 River Rock Drive, Suite 202, Buffalo, New York 14207-2170
Toll-free: 1-800-805-1083   Toll-free fax: 1-800-481-6207
e-mail: gdsinc@genpub.com
www.genpub.com
PUBNET 6307949

CATALOGING IN PUBLICATION DATA

Ross, Nicola, 1957-
Caledon

Includes bibliographical references and index
ISBN 1-55046-301-2

1. Caledon (Ont.). I. Handley, Gord. II. Title

FC3099.C334R67 1999   971.3'535   C99-931705-9
F1059.5.C28R67 1999

Book Design by Walter J. Pick, Taylor Design Group

Printed in Hong Kong by Book Art Inc., Toronto.

THE CANADA COUNCIL | LE CONSEIL DES ARTS
FOR THE ARTS | DU CANADA
SINCE 1957 | DEPUIS 1957

We acknowledge for their financial support of our publishing
program the Canada Council, the Ontario Arts Council, and
the Government of Canada through the Book Publishing
Industry Development Program (BPIDP).

CONTENTS

Maps   6

A Message from the Mayor of Caledon   9

Acknowledgments   11

Foreword   13

Caledon: The Rich Sum of Many Parts   17

There Was an Era When Wheat Was King   21

Across the Credit Forks Trestle and Around the Horseshoe Curve 29

Three Rs by One Room   37

Flyfishing, Freestyle and Fore   43

The Escarpment and the Moraine: A Rough and Rocky Past   49

More Than One Kind of Spirit Haunted Caledon's Inns   57

An Antique Delight   65

There Is Power in Water   71

Over the Escarpment and on to the Trans Canada Trail   79

The Methodists Had Their Appeal   85

An Equine Paradise   93

More Than a Mill for Every Community   101

Naming Those Lines and Sideroads   109

Conclusion   117

Bibliography   119

Index and Photo Credits   120

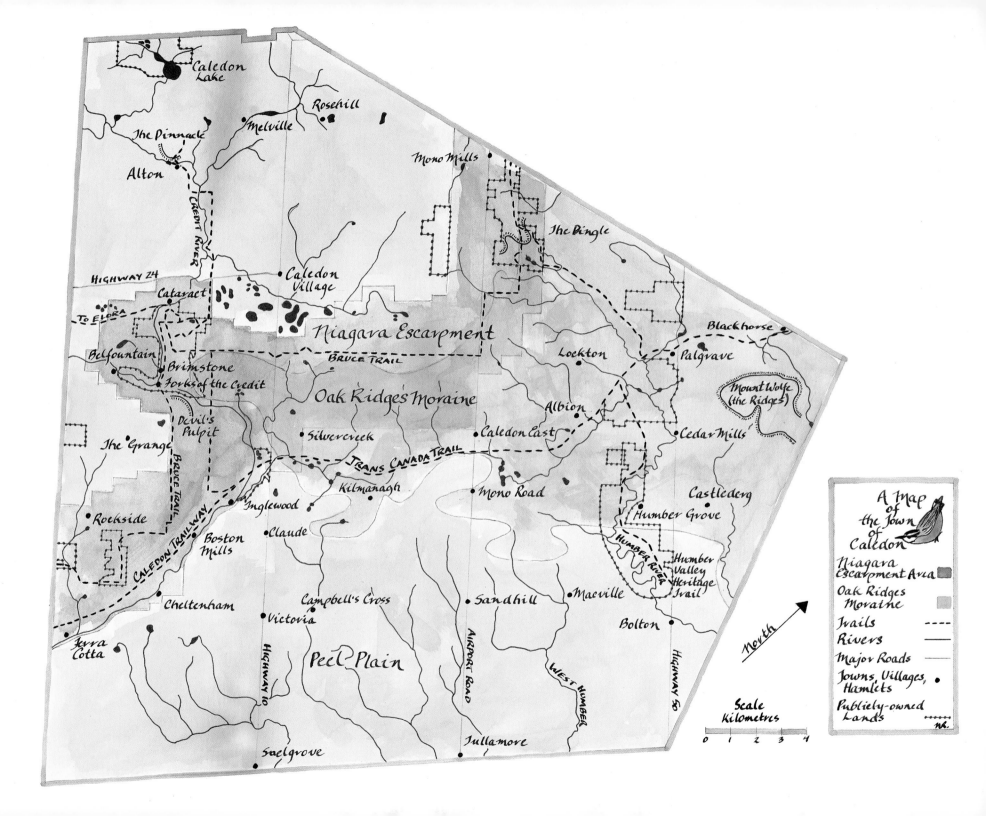

A Map
of
the Town
of Caledon

Niagara Escarpment Area

Oak Ridges Moraine

Trails

Rivers

Major Roads

Towns, Villages, Hamlets

Publicly-owned Lands

Caledon Lake

Rosehill

The Pinnacle

Melville

Alton

Mono Mills

The Dingle

Highway 24

Cataract

Caledon Village

Niagara Escarpment

Blackhorse

Belfountain

Bruce Trail

Lockton

Palgrave

Brimstone

Forks of the Credit

Oak Ridges Moraine

Mount Wolfe (the Ridges)

Devil's Pulpit

Albion

Cedar Mills

The Grange

Silvercreek

Caledon East

Bruce Trail

Trans Canada Trail

Castlederg

Rockside

Caledon Trailway

Kilmanagh

Mono Road

Humber Grove

Inglewood

Boston Mills

Claude

Humber River

Humber Valley Heritage Trail

Cheltenham

Campbell's Cross

Sandhill

Macville

Terra Cotta

Victoria

Bolton

Highway 10

Airport Road

West Humber

Highway 50

Peel Plain

Snelgrove

Tullamore

North

Scale
Kilometres

0 1 2 3 4

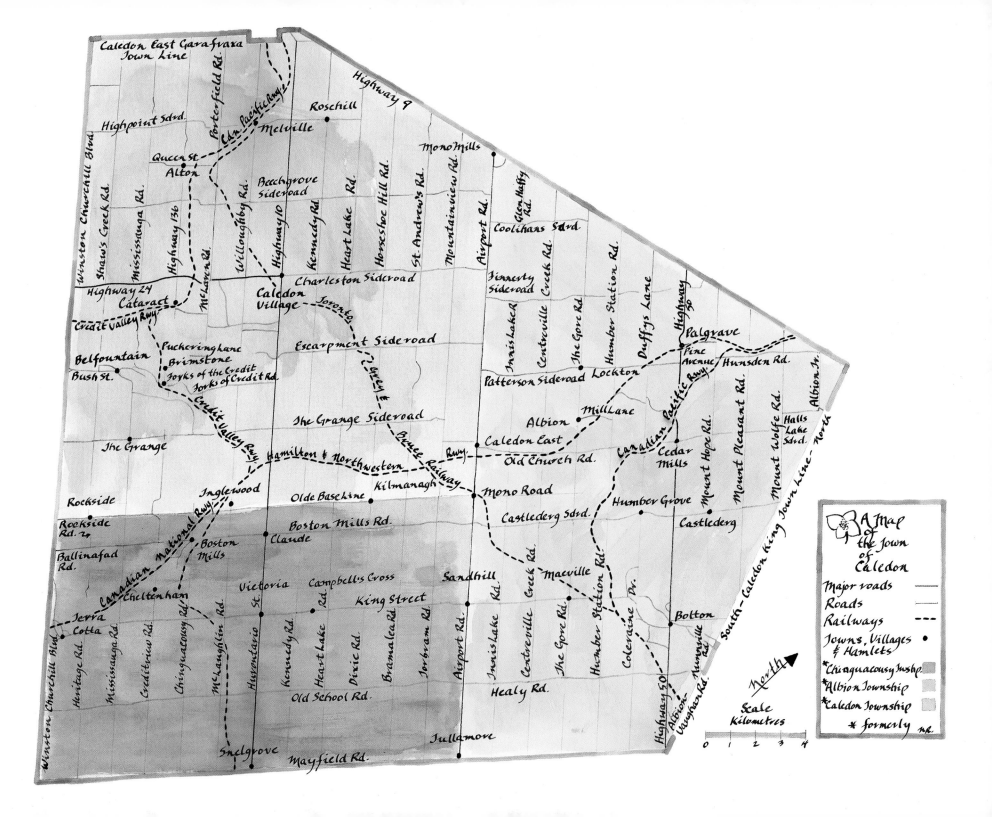

A MESSAGE FROM THE MAYOR OF CALEDON

It is indeed a pleasure to contribute to this fascinating and informative account of the Town of Caledon. I encourage you to venture through the pages of this publication on a journey through our rich past and present.

As a member of Caledon Council since 1988 and mayor since 1994, I have taken much pleasure from my involvement in local government. It has been a personally rewarding and energizing experience. Our government has had many successes and they are contributing to the enjoyment and prosperity of those who live or work in the Town of Caledon and those who visit our beautiful Caledon hills, our picturesque river valleys and quaint towns and villages.

Since the Town of Caledon was formed in 1974 it has grown from a collection of unrelated communities into a strong, distinctive leader of rural municipalities in the Greater Toronto Area. The Town of Caledon is a member of the Region of Peel. Together with our sister municipalities, Mississauga and Brampton, we are working to fulfil our mission to provide an ever-improving level of services for our citizens.

This year, 1999, is our twenty-fifth anniversary. Celebrations marking this milestone will take place throughout the year. We wish to recognize all the people who have worked together to shape present-day Caledon. The five municipalities that were united to form the Town of Caledon in 1974 have each added an interesting dynamic. The rolling picturesque Oak Ridges Moraine is home to the former Township of Albion. The majestic Niagara Escarpment shapes the former Township of Caledon. The bountiful Peel Plain with its productive agricultural lands characterizes the northern half of the former Township of Chinguacousy. The quaint former Village of Caledon East, located at the centre of our municipality, is home to our municipal offices. And finally, the hub of industry and commerce in our municipality continues to be the former Village of Bolton. Over the past twenty-five years we have learned to build on one another's strengths. The result is a rich diversity of lifestyles and opportunities — there is something special for everyone!

Caledon will entice you with a glimpse of our natural assets, our history, industries, villages, towns and lifestyles. Though no book could capture all of Caledon's wonders, *Caledon* brings the past to life and helps us to understand the Caledon of today. This encapsulation of our history reflects the distinctive nature of our community and explains why we have elected to establish our homes and places of business in the Town of Caledon.

On behalf of the people of Caledon, I want to express our appreciation to Nicola Ross, Gord Handley and the Boston Mills Press for providing us with this engaging walk through our past.

The Niagara Escarpment dominates the landscape in parts of Caledon.

Bolton Citizens Band, circa 1930.

Caledon faces new challenges as we move through 1999 and beyond. As a rural municipality in the Greater Toronto Area, we must continue to be good custodians of our lands and resources. We need to protect our villages, green open spaces and our rural quality of life. We have curtailed urban-type development in the Town of Caledon by limiting it to specific areas. This allows small towns to grow and prosper as they provide centralized services for the benefit of all the communities within Caledon. At the same time, our rural areas can continue to support agriculture, recreational pursuits, ecological diversity and some of the most desirable living conditions possible. We are truly blessed by Caledon's bounty.

Our next twenty-five years will bring new challenges, new partnerships and new opportunities. I look forward to being part of the future and to working together with the people of Caledon to steward our lands and communities, to safeguard the precious rural lifestyle that we enjoy, and to develop a municipality that continues to be desirable, vibrant and viable.

Mayor Carol Seglins
Caledon
July 1999

ACKNOWLEDGMENTS

The research undertaken for a project such as this book takes the researcher to all sorts of unexpected places. New acquaintances are made and friendships created. It's an excuse that allows the researcher to meet so many fascinating people and visit so many wonderful landmarks. It's an opportunity to be wowed by the willingness of others to help out and participate.

Annie Dillard wrote:
"We are here to witness creation
and abet it.
We are here to notice each thing
so that each thing is noticed."

The following people abet creation and notice so many things. Many thanks to the Boston Mills Press, Neil Bird, Heather Broadbent, Lou Dryden, Gord Handley, Alex and June Raeburn, Oakland Ross, Barry Westhouse, my Mum and, of course, Caledon herself.

FOREWORD

The amalgamation of all the municipalities and communities of north Peel, some twenty-five years ago, has in no way dimmed the mystique and allure of this place, Caledon. That union gives the new town attractive and interesting sections of those most outstanding Southern Ontario landforms: the Niagara Escarpment and the Oak Ridges Moraine.

From their shared headwaters on our northern boundary, our two rivers, the Humber and the Credit, though small by some standards, played a major part in the development of Caledon. It is stirring now to witness the attention that many of our younger people are giving to improving the health of these waterways.

Both of us have known Caledon for just about half the time since the first settlers arrived. In fact, our great-grandparents were among those first homesteaders. Our eighty-some years have probably seen more of the changes that have affected the lives and the lifestyles of our people than any other period since time began. Communication, transportation, education, the food we eat and how we obtain it — all have changed, from our wire-fence telephone system to the cell phone, the horse rig to autos, walking up to three miles to that one-room school in summer, and then in winter, when you arrived to find your ink bottle frozen solid and wore your overcoat until noon.

The geology of the area seems to have been fairly well studied, but very little of the actual history and hardship of the people of early Caledon and how they adapted to change has ever been recorded. Those early residents are the ones to whom we must give full credit for preserving such a wondrous natural heritage. And through their efforts and through all these years, almost untarnished, the allure of Caledon remains.

In the pages of this book, you'll discover the story of many of the people and the events that have kept Caledon "a great place to live."

June and Alex Raeburn
Alton, Ontario
November 1998

CALEDON: THE RICH SUM OF MANY PARTS

You can wrap yourself up in Caledon. Like a favourite blanket, it makes you feel safe and at home. But the fabric of Caledon varies. Hardly noticeable at first, the differences become more apparent the closer you look. In fact, the Town of Caledon is the result of an amalgamation of the Townships of Caledon, Albion and the northern part of Chinguacousy as well as the villages of Bolton and Caledon East. And each of these regions — brought together in 1974 not by nature but by man's law — has a unique character.

The northwest, formerly Caledon Township, is bounded by Winston Churchill Boulevard, Olde Base Line, Airport Road and the Caledon East Garafraxa Town Line. The Niagara Escarpment and the Credit River dominate this area. Its rich water and mineral resources attracted settlers and early industrialists. Referred to in the past as "one of the best mill streams in Ontario," the mighty Credit once supported nineteen mills within Caledon's borders. In the earliest settlement days, however, pioneers had no access to this tremendous source of power. In 1806, when the Mississauga Indians gave up the first portion of the Mississauga Tract, they exchanged 35,000 hectares of Lake Ontario's shoreline for £1,000 in goods, but they kept the Credit River. The Mississauga held on to the land for one and a half kilometres on either side of this important waterway. It wasn't until 1818 that they gave up this right by surrendering an additional 262,000 hectares, including access to the river, and all of what is now the Town of Caledon, for an annual payment of £522 10p in goods.

The first European settlers came in 1818 and legend has it that they came in search of gold. In those days, the trip to Caledon or, more precisely, the Forks of the Credit area, led only to a glitter of hope and cost more than one adventurer his life. No gold was ever found. But so began a long period of industrial development. By some accounts, the Credit River back then flowed at a rate that was

The doctors' house in Bolton.

17

Only the foundation of this octagonal barn can be found today.

as much as one hundred times greater than today's sedate pace. To exploit the river's tremendous power, settlers began erecting sawmills, grist mills, woollen mills and power plants. They built stone quarries, bottling plants, breweries and distilleries.

The earliest frame and log buildings put up by pioneers near the Credit in Caledon's northwest were soon replaced by stone and sometimes brick structures that were stronger, less prone to fire — and denoted affluence. Villages became prosperous bustling centres, many of them more active in the 1880s than they are today. These communities followed the Credit's path. They were often tucked close to the Niagara Escarpment that supplied the limestone used to build houses and barns, schoolhouses, churches, hotels, mills, fences and stores. The land was often too hilly or gravelly to support more than subsistence agriculture, so farms remained small.

Today, Alton, Inglewood, Cheltenham, Belfountain, Cataract, Brimstone and Terra Cotta are picturesque little villages and hamlets.

(Terra Cotta and Cheltenham are actually located in Chinguacousy Township, however, they share many of Caledon Township's characteristics.) What remains of the industries these locations once supported have either been destroyed or renovated into stores and restaurants, inns and homes. Tourism has taken over as visitors flock to see Caledon's sights, to shop, hike, fish, or simply enjoy the fresh country air. At the same time, a lot of people just live here. A few farm, but agriculture in Caledon's northwest is difficult.

That is not the case a little further south in what was the northern portion of Chinguacousy Township, a tract of land that also became part of the Town of Caledon back in 1974. Including the area south of Olde Base Line and north of Mayfield Road, between Winston Churchill Boulevard and Airport Road, this region is blessed with some of the finest agricultural soil in Southern Ontario.

The Belfountain Village Store.

Once the land had been cleared, farmers revered its plain-like flatness and rich soil. Wheat, the golden crop of the mid-1800s, grew in field upon field. Original log and frame houses were quickly replaced with the magnificent brick houses that interrupt today's lush fields of corn. Many Chinguacousy farmers had money to spare and they used it to build wonderful homes. The fine brickwork, cornice mouldings, gingerbreading and other architectural details found in these houses as well as the massive, solid barns hint at the wealth the land brought to Chinguacousy farmers, particularly those who lived on the Peel Plain that runs through this section.

Albion Township is different again. Taking up the area bounded by Airport Road and the Caledon King Town Line (and the Albion Vaughan Road) between Highway 9 and Mayfield Road, its dozens of streams that flow into the Humber River give the landscape a very distinctive feel. Albion Township is not dominated by the rocky cliffs of the Niagara Escarpment; rather, it scales the Oak Ridges Moraine. From the Moraine's greatest heights, the land seems to fall away forever. The vistas from above Caledon East and Palgrave bear no resemblance to the nooks and crannies of Caledon Township or the flatlands of Chinguacousy.

In much of Albion, the soil was rich but very sandy. After its trees had been felled, Albion suffered more than other regions of Caledon. The winds blew away the topsoil. Exposed sand piled up in dunes and roads had to be ploughed to free them of this nuisance. It was no accident that Sandhill was called by this name. Albion strained to support commercial agriculture and the settlers here were seldom able to replace their earliest homes. As a result, Albion now boasts dozens of log homes, many of them lovingly refurbished yet hidden within forest regrowth and small agricultural fields.

An early log house near Caledon East.

The Humber River had its impact. While agricultural practices in the northern parts of Albion were largely limited to subsistence farming, the southern areas below the Oak Ridges Moraine were more fertile. First settled in about 1820, Bolton prospered once its water-powered grist mill came on line. Today, Bolton is a booming town where small industry abounds and some 15,000 of Caledon's residents reside.

These three regions maintain their separate identities even now. Yet all parts of the Town of Caledon were settled by the same Irish, Scottish and English immigrants and by United Empire Loyalists from the United States. Much of the land was also divvied up among soldiers and officers returning from the War of 1812. It was mostly the whim of the Commissioner of Crown Lands in York that caused homesteaders to settle where they did in Albion or Chinguacousy or Caledon Township. Nonetheless, longtime residents remain fiercely loyal to their particular locale — they stick to the old names. They'll insist that they live on the Third Line of Albion even though it's now called Centreville Creek Road. And it's surprising how many people in the old Chinguacousy Township are unaware that Bolton is even part of Caledon. Residents of Belfountain may never have visited Palgrave or seen the vistas from atop the Mount Wolfe ridge. Those who reside in Snelgrove might well need directions to find Alton.

So when the time came to amalgamate in 1974, the challenge of choosing a name for the combined area was the subject of considerable — let us say — debate. It was finally put to a referendum. Three names were on the ballot: Albion (from the township of the same name), Caledon (also from the township) and Cardwell, from the name of the local federal electoral district (from 1867 to 1900) that was named after an English parliamentarian, Viscount Cardwell. Caledon won out, but it would

have been as fitting had Albion been victorious. After all, Caledon is the poetic name for Scotland while Albion is the romantic name for Mother England. (Erin, located in Wellington County, is the romantic name for Ireland.)

Still, it was "Caledon" that carried the day, and so it is "Caledon" that appears in the title of this book. In the end, however, a volume of this scope cannot pretend to describe every aspect of Caledon's rich history, its wealth of stories, its landmarks and scenery, its legions of fascinating people. For every church discussed and schoolhouse mentioned, two more begged to be included. Whole books could have been written about Caledon's log houses or its horses. Many more pages could have been filled describing each town and village. It seems almost a crime to limit agriculture to a single chapter. But there is only so much that can be crammed into the pages of a single book, and that is surely a tribute to the distinctive qualities of the area — its incredible richness and diversity. In the text and photographs that follow, you will at least be able to sample those qualities. If you still want more, you'll have to come to Caledon yourself. If you are already here, enjoy.

THERE WAS AN ERA WHEN WHEAT WAS KING

As the twentieth century winds down, the Town of Caledon has become more of a place where people live than a place where people work and live. Two-thirds of Caledon's resident workforce is employed outside its borders. Jobs within Caledon are shared about equally between those who live here and those who do not.

This situation differs markedly from Caledon's earlier days. During the first half of the nineteenth century, as settlers began arriving, keeping your family fed and sheltered took up the entire day and then some. Esther Heyes describes the hard life of an early settler in her book, *The Story of Albion*. (Albion Township became part of the Town of Caledon in 1974.)

"Once located, the settler started in to do battle with the forest. When the first spring came round he was ready to plant a small crop, usually potatoes and a little Indian corn, along with squashes and pumpkins, around the stumps of his initial clearing. No cultivating was done. Time could be spent to better advantage clearing more land, and the freshly uncovered soil was rich enough and free enough from weeds to give a good return without much work.

"Fall wheat was sown among the stumps on additional land cleared during the first summer… The next year spring wheat was sown where corn and potatoes had been… After four or five years the tree roots in the earliest clearing would have

Harvesting grain near Cheltenham, circa 1920.

disintegrated sufficiently for the farmer to do some primitive plough-ing, and another crop of wheat would be taken off, followed again by oats or rye or pasture. Finally, after about ten years of settlement the stumps could be pulled by oxen, and the wide cleared fields taken into permanent, methodical cultivation."

Subsistence agriculture predominated until the 1850s. At this juncture, several events pushed Caledon's farmers toward commercial farming. First, the prices of agricultural commodities, especially wheat, were jacked up by the California gold rush (1849). Furthermore, crops failed in Europe at the same time as the

Crimean War (1854–56) cut off the supply of Russian wheat. In 1855, wheat from Ontario was selling for $2.40 per bushel. This compared with a low of about thirty-two cents per bushel in 1832. Many of Caledon's fine farmhouses and barns were built on the proceeds from wheat during these prosperous years.

About this time, farmers also learned how to harness animal power to speed up harvesting. This meant farmers' productivity was no longer totally dependent upon the number of farm hands available. Finally, improved farm practices promoted by provincial agricultural associations began having a positive effect on productivity.

A reciprocity treaty signed with the United States came into effect in 1854 and lasted until 1865. It encouraged Ontario farmers to diversify. Barley was in high demand by American breweries and mixed farming appeared. The quality of local cattle began improving with the arrival of the first purebreds. By the time the treaty was removed, local cattle breeders had made dramatic improvements to their stock. By the 1870s there was a healthy demand for local cattle outside North America. Dairy farming also picked up in the 1850s, as did hog production.

During this period one of Caledon's leading farmers was J. C. Snell. At one time he was growing over 200 hectares of wheat on his farm near the corner of Highway 10 and Mayfield Road. It was all cut by hand. He began breeding Shorthorns in 1855 and also purchased a Cotswold ram and ewe. He added Berkshire swine and latter imported Galloway cattle, Yorkshire and Suffolk swine and Southdown sheep. Snell's sons kept up their father's tradition of excellence after his death. Between 1878 and 1884 they won more prizes at the Chicago Fat Stock Show than any other Canadian exhibitor. Consequently, it's not surprising that when their local village, Edmonton, was asked by the post office to change its name, it became known as Snelgrove.

While the 1880s were a time of frenzied quarrying in some parts of Caledon, it was agriculture that ruled Peel County as a whole. By then a larger percentage of land had been cleared in Peel than in any other county in Ontario. By 1900 more than ninety percent of Peel's tree cover had been removed and almost sixty percent of the wetlands had been drained, mostly so the land could be used for farming. But just as a rich agricultural future seemed sure, events — natural and human — came along to challenge agriculture's dominance. Commodity prices fell as the West opened up to farming and Ontario slid into the "Sixty-Year Doldrums," a recession that spanned the years 1890 to 1950. Furthermore, overproduction of wheat and the loss of tree cover meant that the soil wasn't just exhausted — it began to blow away.

Near Cheltenham.

The Haines still live by the Haines Mill in Cheltenham.

Much of Caledon's soil, especially in Albion Township, was very fine. Without trees, the wind played havoc with farmers' newly cultivated fields. Huge dunes formed, and parts of Airport Road had to be ploughed to keep them clear of sand. In an effort to stem this sandy tide, the provincial government initiated tree-planting programs, but parts of Caledon would never live up to the farming potential some had dreamed of.

The number of farms in Peel County decreased during the early part of the twentieth century. The lure of the West stole many young men and women away, and the First World War (1914–18) meant that farm labour was in short supply. This manpower shortage spurred on the trend toward mechanization. The Ontario government introduced tractors during the war, and electricity arrived, much to the delight of farm women. Farm organizations such as the Ontario Department of Agriculture's Extension Service, 4H and Women's Institutes improved agricultural practices and contributed

to the social fabric of rural areas such as Caledon. Nonetheless, between 1901 and 1961, the number of farms in Peel County decreased from 13,687 to 6,600. The downward trend continues today. In 1981 there were 626 farms in the Town of Caledon. Fifteen years later, in 1996, there were only 490.

But despite the loss of farms, 1963 was a banner year for local agriculture. In October of that year, Caledon hosted the agricultural world at the World Ploughing Match. The Right Honourable Lester B. Pearson, prime minister of Canada, opened the event, held on the farm of Connie Smythe near Caledon Village. Some eighteen countries entered, including Central Africa, Denmark, Finland, France, New Zealand and the United States. Attendance topped all previous World Ploughing Matches and it was deemed a great success by all who partook. Today, a Cairn of Peace commemorates the 1963 World Ploughing Match. Located in front of

Barns such as the one being built here, circa 1920, dot the countryside.

The Ploughing Match, Chinguacousy Township, circa 1920.

Caledon Village Place, it is one of a number of similar cairns around that world that "promote peace and unity."

It was fitting that Caledon hosted this prestigious event since it has some of Ontario's finest agricultural land. The vast flatland known as the Peel Plain, especially on the east side of Highway 10, south of Olde Base Line, is dotted with well-maintained barns and silos. Lush cornfields straddle country roads and the quality of more-than-century-old brick and stone farmhouses, many adorned with architectural details that only the wealthy could afford, attest to the region's rich agricultural heritage. Surprisingly,

a second pocket of premiere farmland sits to the northeast of Caledon Village, perched on the Niagara Escarpment.

In 1996, gross farm receipts from Caledon's 490 farms were $47 million. Mixed or miscellaneous farms, cattle operations and dairy herds topped the list of farm types. Specialty crops such as canola, soya beans and sunflowers now complement corn, oats and hay. Apples and other fruits and vegetables are not uncommon and they have contributed to the growing trend of farmer markets. For years, the old "Sales Barn" just north of Snelgrove has provided local residents with an opportunity to buy fresh fruits and vegetables as well as pigs, sheep and cattle. Direct-from-the-farm outlets are ever more popular with local residents and in one case, a market has become a tourist attraction. On autumn weekends there are almost as many cars in the parking lot at Downey's on Heart Lake Road as there are pumpkins. A pumpkin "tree" lights the nighttime sky and pony rides help make buying farm-fresh produce and home-baked goods an adventure for everyone in the family.

Diminishing farm numbers and Downey's success illustrate just how much Caledon has changed since its European settlers first arrived. Today, while aggregate extraction and agriculture remain significant areas of employment, many people now have jobs in tourism and the service industry. Inns and restaurants, antique and gift stores employ hundreds. Tourists crowd Belfountain and other villages each weekend eating ice cream, peeking into shops and gazing at the marvellous works of art prepared by Caledon's growing arts community. Galleries and studios grace most of Caledon's hamlets. Local artisans — painters, woodworkers, sculptors, ironmongers and more — open up their homes and studios to the public for autumn tours.

Caledon's hiking trails, parks and conservation areas attract even more visitors. Annual events such as the Caledon and Bolton Fall Fairs and other community initiatives bring entire families that may stay for a day or a weekend. The Caledon Ski Club, fishing clubs, cycling clubs, an archery club, golf clubs and more do healthy business and are significant local employers. Caledon's spectacular scenery, the wildflowers, wildlife and autumn colours also do their share in making the area a destination.

But nowhere in Caledon have employment opportunities blossomed as they have in Bolton. During the ten-year span between 1981 and 1991, the number of jobs in Caledon grew by more than seventy percent (from 6,675 to 11,485) and the majority of them appeared in Bolton. The population of this once-sleepy little community almost tripled to about 15,000 over the same period, making it far and away the largest centre in Caledon. The next biggest is Caledon East, the home of the Town of Caledon's government offices, where only 2,300 people reside.

Bolton's proximity to rail and air transport, Brampton, Toronto and the United States makes it an ideal location for light manufacturers and other businesses to set up shop. Between 1994 and 1997, some 164 new companies opened up in Caledon, the majority of them making Bolton their home.

One of Bolton's most impressive corporations is Husky Injection Molding Systems Ltd. This company began in president Robert Schad's garage in the 1950s. He moved his operation to Bolton in 1968 and now, some thirty years later, customers in seventy countries spend more than US$762 million on the products Husky makes. The company employs over 2,800 people, almost sixty percent of them in Bolton. There they build the machines that make injection moulds for products such as plastic pop bottles, automotive parts and laptop computer housings.

Much of this activity takes place within Husky's 24-hectare Bolton "campus." Behind the low earthen berms that separate Husky from Highway 50 lies a naturalized park-like setting that resembles no other industrial facility in Canada. Husky's five modern office and industrial buildings, daycare and wellness centre and parking area are surrounded and separated by tall grasses, wild and propagated flowers and trees. A small waterfall cascades into a pond where runoff from Husky's storm sewers is naturally cleansed. Ducks and fish inhabit this oasis that is overlooked by

At Downey's fruit and vegetable market the entire family is entertained.

the company's health food cafeteria. The rule is "no grass" and no accompanying pesticides, mowers or herbicides. Recipient of the 1998 Financial Post Gold Award in Environmental Leadership and the 1995 Lieutenant-Governor's Conservation Award, Husky is truly a leader in responsible care.

The recently created Schad Foundation brings a new dimension to the company. With its mandate to support local, national and international environmental and health initiatives, it is one of Canada's largest and most generous environmental donors. The example set by this philanthropic approach to business and to life fits well with Husky's grand surroundings in Caledon.

Husky Injection Molding in Bolton is recognized for its environmental leadership.

ACROSS THE CREDIT FORKS TRESTLE & AROUND THE HORSESHOE CURVE

Caledon, the ebb and flow of her communities, her economic booms and busts, her very identity, cannot be separated from the railway. So influential was the arrival — or non-arrival — of the iron horse that often it separated those communities that rose to prominence from those that slid into oblivion. Villages such as Inglewood and Cataract were particularly fortunate. Not only were they blessed with rich natural resources, they were also at the junction of more than one rail line. Commerce and industry in these centres boomed around the turn of the century because of their rail links. Mono Mills, Claude and Silvercreek, on the other hand, were bypassed. They suffered slow declines as their inhabitants moved away, taking their enterprises with them.

But the arrival of the train was not always a good thing. Business in Bolton was eroded by this new mode of transportation. Access to the railway meant that once-distant Brampton and Toronto were now close by. So too were the less costly and more abundant supplies and services found in these large centres.

Although the Canadian Pacific and Canadian National railway empires eventually scooped up all three of Caledon's original railways, they started out as privately owned independent operations. Starting in the late 1800s, the Credit Valley Railway traversed Caledon's hills. Stops in Ferndale, Inglewood, the Forks of the Credit, Cataract, Alton and Melville marked the train's journey from Streetsville to Orangeville. At Cataract a branch line provided service to Erin, Hillsburgh and Elora. The Hamilton & Northwestern Railway linked Hamilton to Collingwood by passing through Terra Cotta, Boston Mills, Cheltenham, Inglewood, Caledon East and Palgrave. At Cardwell Junction, a point southwest of Caledon East, the Toronto, Grey & Bruce Railway passed over the Hamilton & Northwestern line on its way from Toronto to Orangeville and points beyond. It visited stations in Bolton, Mono Road, Caledon Village and Melville and included the famous Horseshoe Curve.

Mono Road was once a main stop along the Toronto, Grey & Bruce Railway.

While the Hamilton & Northwestern Railway ran through Palgrave it was a booming town. The H&NW is now the Caledon Trailway.

The charter for the Credit Valley Railway (CVR) was signed in 1871. But it didn't make it to Inglewood until 1879, two years after the Hamilton & Northwestern Railway (H&NW) appeared. The CVR's arrival in Inglewood was delayed by two local property-owners who blocked construction on their land until the CVR paid up in full. It also arrived after its owners had niggled hefty "bonuses" from the towns and municipalities along its route. Charters may have awarded rights to build railways, but no money was provided. This gave rise to all sorts of "deals." These bonuses helped determine which towns did and which towns did not end up with a railway stop.

Construction of the CVR, especially of the original wooden trestle at the Forks of the Credit, was an engineering feat unequalled at the time. Some 350 metres in length, the trestle was the longest wooden curved trestle in Ontario. The 26-metre-high bridge incorporated over 150,000 metres of lumber and its construction required the services of 250 men and 50 teams of horses. It turned almost a full 90 degrees as it crossed the West Credit River. In 1886, the trestle was reinforced. A shuttle train that ran between Cataract and the Forks of the Credit simply dumped earth between the legs of the trestle until much of it had been filled in and strengthened.

In the mind of its founder, George Laidlaw, the Credit Valley Railway was going to make its fortune transporting cordwood to satisfy Toronto's enormous appetite for fuel. In reality, however, after only four years, the financially ailing CVR was sold. It was picked up by the Ontario & Quebec Railway Co., a precursor to the Canadian Pacific Railway. This meant that as of 1883, the

The Cheltenham railway station was moved to a private residence. It is the only one in Caledon that was not demolished.

31

Ontario & Quebec Railway was at the helm of both the Toronto Gore & Bruce (TG&B) line that ran from Toronto through Bolton to Orangeville and the CVR line with its route from Streetsville to Orangeville. The two lines met at Melville, so in 1884, the CPR closed the five kilometres of CVR tracks between Melville and Orangeville and routed all trains on to the TG&B line. This was the first railway line to be abandoned in Ontario — and a premonition of things to come.

Regular passenger service was offered on the CVR route. One of two daily return trains left Streetsville at 5:20 PM, hit the Forks of the Credit at 6:32 PM and ended up in Orangeville at 7:02 PM. Sadly, service gradually diminished until only a dayliner, consisting of a combined diesel engine and passenger car, came along three times a week. This decline meant that many towns lost their stationmasters and their station houses. They were reduced to flag stops. Eventually, as more and more automobiles made their way

The wooden trestle in the Credit Forks, circa 1888. It took 250 men aided by 50 teams of horses to build it.

up to Caledon, the demand for rail service diminished until all passenger train service along the CVR ceased in 1970.

It's still possible to experience the wonder of seeing a freight train cross over the now steel-and-concrete-reinforced trestle in the Forks of the Credit, but it only happens on alternate weekdays. But in the late 1990s, Canadian Pacific Railway put the line up for sale. Whether this spectacular railway is picked up by local municipalities or meets the same fate as the stations that no longer grace Caledon's villages remains to be seen.

By 1883, the Ontario & Quebec Railway Co. owned both the CVR and the TG&B even though they had started out as competitors. Passengers boarding the TG&B in Toronto could travel to Owen Sound. Once there, the Owen Sound Steamship Company sailed to Thunder Bay and Sault Ste. Marie. In this way, the TG&B line through Caledon connected Toronto with the transcontinental rail line and Western Canada. For this reason, and because its terminus was Toronto, the Ontario & Quebec Railway ran its prestigious express service along the TG&B.

This route sounds grand, but the TG&B had problems from the moment its first train arrived in Orangeville in 1871. It was built as a narrow-gauge line to save money, but this misguided decision was an immediate problem. Narrow-gauge trains couldn't pull much of a load and the TG&B wasn't able to keep up with demand. Freight sat for days on station platforms and when it finally arrived in Toronto, extra costs were incurred to transfer it to standard-gauge trains. In 1881, some ten years after the first train travelled this route, all the rails were pulled up and replaced with standard gauge. Furthermore, curves, grades and bridges had to be altered and new locomotives and cars purchased. Any savings from the narrow gauge quickly vanished.

Another questionable decision of the TG&B involved the famous Horseshoe Curve. This switchback turn allowed trains to climb up the 120-metre Niagara Escarpment. From Mile 37 south to Mile 38 north, trains climbed 26 metres in less than a half a kilometre. There is little evidence today of this curve, located at a point west of Horseshoe Hill Road and just south of Escarpment Sideroad, or of the famous accident that occurred there. But back at the turn of the century the spot was well known.

On September 5, 1907, a train loaded with almost 150 passengers left Orangeville, having come from points north. It was bound for the Toronto Exhibition. The seven-car train never arrived at its destination. Instead, it ended up a tangled mess of mangled wood and metal after jumping the tracks at the Horseshoe Curve. The train's engineer and conductor were charged with criminal negligence as a result of this tragedy that killed 7 and injured 114. And though theory has it that the crash

Inglewood, at the junction of the CVR and the H&NW, circa 1900.

was caused by excessive speed, both men were acquitted. Despite this horrific accident and the robbery that occurred in 1906 after thieves boarded the train at Cardwell Junction, the TG&B continued to operate until 1931. Two years later the 30 kilometres of track between Bolton and Melville were pulled up and the right-of-way turned over to local landowners. This made the TG&B Caledon's second rail line to be dismantled.

The third cog in Caledon's railway network was the Hamilton & Northwestern Railway (H&NW). The City of Hamilton built the railway in hopes of keeping up with its neighbour around the bay. Toronto had the Northern Railway that ran to Barrie. Hamilton wanted a competing line. Both were in pursuit of a link with the transcontinental railway project at Lake Nipissing. However, money to build the H&NW was raised by convincing communities between Hamilton, Barrie and Collingwood that

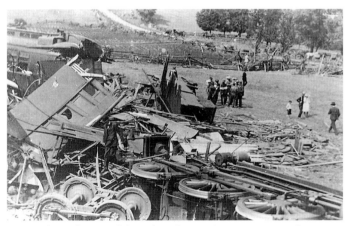

In 1907 the TG&B jumped the tracks at the Horseshoe Curve. Some 114 were injured and 7 died in the crash.

competition for the Northern would mean lower freight and passenger rates. The H&NW promised that, "under no circumstances shall the said Railway be transferred or placed under the control of any other Railway Company." Nonetheless, some six months after arriving in Collingwood in December, 1878, the H&NW formed an alliance with the Northern Railway, a partnership forced upon them by tough economic times.

The Grand Trunk Railway sat in waiting as the partnership unravelled. By the mid-1880s, the Montreal-based Grand Trunk had picked up the H&NW and by 1922 the Grand Trunk had been gobbled up by the Canadian National Railway.

Today, the local H&NW line is more commonly known as the Caledon Trailway, a 33-kilometre footpath that traverses the Town of Caledon and is part of the Trans Canada Trail. But before its conversion to a hiking trail, trains crossed the border into Caledon just north of the village of Terra Cotta. Developed as a railway town, Terra Cotta bustled with activity after the

Visible along the Caledon Trailway near Caledon East, this bridge is the spot where the TG&B passed over the H&NW.

train's arrival. This transportation link spurred on local industry, since the village was now connected with its markets. Limestone and sandstone were hauled out of its quarries, bricks were made from its red clay, and the Credit River that ran through the village provided power for mills and electricity generation. Stores, hotels and other services sprang up as people settled in the village.

Over time, the train stopped at one of three railway stations, the earliest of which was graced with the name Salmonville. Terra Cotta, like so many of Caledon's communities, had its name changed from time to time. Before Salmonville was popularized, it was known as Tucker's Mill and even Plewes' Mills. Sadly, all three of the village's railway stations burned down, the last one in 1956. By that time, demand for Terra Cotta's products had waned and the station was never rebuilt.

As the train made its way from Terra Cotta to Cheltenham it passed by the "Cheltenham brickyards." Built by the Interprovincial Brick Company, the site produced 90,000 bricks per day at its peak. Whereas Terra Cotta was incorporated in 1891, some seventeen years after the HN&W passed through, Cheltenham was in existence long before the train arrived. Incorporated as early as 1837, Cheltenham was named after the British city of the same name. Cheltenham's station house is the only one in Caledon that has survived. An insightful resident moved it to his home. There is no trace, however, of the grain elevator that used to be by its side.

The line then passed through the flag stop of Boston Mills en route to Inglewood, where it crossed the CVR tracks. Inglewood, another pre-railway village, nonetheless benefited from its railways. Its woollen mill and quarries made great use of rail transportation. Inglewood's original wooden "union" station was so named, in part, because it was at the union of two rail lines. Sadly, it was destroyed by fire around 1910. Until it was replaced by a yellow brick station, the stationmaster worked from an old boxcar. The brick version and its water tower were demolished in 1972, several years after service along the line had ceased.

The next stop along the line, after it crossed under the TG&B bridge at Cardwell Junction, was Caledon East. Here, the transformation from quarrying to agriculture was complete. In *The Story of Albion,* Esther Heyes reports that in front of the Caledon East station, farmers' wagons, loaded with potatoes, cattle or grain, often lined up for as far as the eye could see.

Further east, Centreville, officially renamed Albion in 1907, was once a stop. Hardly evident today, Centreville had a post office, a blacksmith's shop and an inn in the late 1800s. It also had a station house, though that was yet another sad casualty of a 1960s demolition crew.

Finally, before leaving Caledon's eastern border, the train passed through Palgrave, where its presence prompted construction of a stockyard, elevator and potato-grading facility. An enlarged H&NW style Number 3 station house served Palgrave until it too burned down in 1918. And, as was the case in so many other towns and villages, the station that replaced it was dismantled after the line was taken out of service.

Though Caledon's rail history is based upon conventional railways, it was very nearly quite different. Had the TG&B train not passed through Caledon in 1871, the Orangeville tramway might have been constructed. Plans to build a horse-drawn tramway on wooden rails to connect Orangeville to Brampton along Hurontario Street (Highway 10) were well underway by 1870. In fact, in 1867, work began on the first five kilometres

If you are patient, you too might see a freight train cross over the trestle in the Credit Forks.

south of Orangeville. D. Neufeld, who focused on Caledon in his unpublished report entitled, "The Impact of Technological and Business Innovation on a Nineteenth Century Frontier: A Case Study in Central Ontario," believes failure to build this tramway was a mistake. He wrote, "Thus, in the loss of the Orangeville Tramway Company, the area surrendered the initiative of local development to Toronto entrepreneurs and gave up control of its own destiny."

Whether having a locally controlled tramway would have changed development in Caledon will never be known for certain. But lack of cooperation from large rail companies was certainly a factor in the loss of Caledon's steam train to the South Simcoe Railway in Tottenham.

In 1971, local rail enthusiasts in Caledon embarked on their dream of bringing a steam train back to Ontario. Their vision seemed to be fulfilled when, on May 19, 1973, the gleaming, ex-CPR ten-wheeler, Number 1057, emerged. Resplendent in her new black paint, with white trim and nickel and brass fixtures, she was christened *Credit Valley*. Passenger cars had been reconditioned to their former glory. Each bore the name of a different stop in the Credit Valley — Cataract, Forks of the Credit, Chinguacousy, Cheltenham, Terra Cotta. The inaugural run of

the iron horse through Caledon on its journey from Toronto to Owen Sound was sold out months in advance. And indeed, on May 27, 1973, it performed beautifully for all its fans. At every possible vantage point along its route, hundreds of spectators waved and cheered Number 1057 on.

The steam train made a number of journeys along this route. But negotiations to have permanent access to the unused portion of the CN line (formerly the H&NW line) between Cheltenham and Georgetown failed and the Credit Valley and all of her passenger cars were consequently sold to the South Simcoe Railway. Today, the only evidence of Caledon's steam train is the old turntable that was transported from Elora to the Cheltenham brickyards when it appeared the *Credit Valley* would remain an integral part of Caledon.

And though many dreams died when the *Credit Valley* moved to Tottenham, train travel in Caledon isn't completely a thing of the past. The CPR makes limited use of the old CVR line through the Forks of the Credit. Furthermore, CPR's mainline runs through the southeastern portion of the Town of Caledon. Up to thirty freight trains per day use this route. And though they never stop to pick up passengers, they do blow their whistles — and help keep train transportation alive in Caledon.

THREE Rs BY ONE ROOM

The benefits of a unified Canada are in some doubt today. But back in 1841, the union of Upper and Lower Canada brought a free, well-organized, public education system to places such as Caledon. Previously, there had been no local access to formal education. Only fortunate children — though they might not have felt very lucky — received any training in the three Rs.

With formalized public education came the need for schools. None of the earliest log structures built to serve this purpose have survived. But many of the redbrick and limestone schoolhouses that replaced them still dot our countryside. Their borders of sugar maples make old schools easy to pick out. These ample trees stand as regularly spaced sentries still ready to protect Caledon's youth.

In the 1960s, School Sections were replaced by amalgamated Township School Boards. They built new, larger schools with multiple classrooms, indoor plumbing, central heating and gymnasiums to replace one-room schools. Bus routes were set up to carry students to these modern facilities. As a result, Caledon's one-room schoolhouses were boarded up and sold at auction to the highest bidder.

Chinguacousy Township closed up thirteen one-room schoolhouses, Albion Township shut down twelve, and the old Township of Caledon ceased to use sixteen. Tragically, after being sold, many of these heritage buildings were destroyed or irrevocably altered to accommodate cars, welding businesses or other seemingly inappro-

priate tenants. The reason more were not converted into residences — a logical means of preservation — stems from a sad fact. Since neither Chinguacousy nor Albion Townships had bylaws to govern the satisfactory conversion of schoolhouses into residences, they outlawed this practice. Redbrick or stone, it didn't matter. They were all auctioned off but could be used only for storage or other nonresidential purposes. Fortunately, the old Township of Caledon either had no similar stipulation or didn't enforce it. Consequently, many, though not all, well-preserved schoolhouses are clustered in the northwest portion of today's Town of Caledon.

So numerous were the schoolhouses along one road in Chinguacousy Township that it came to be called Old School Road. Of the three that remain today (there were seven), one is the lovely Sharpe Schoolhouse. It escaped conversion to a garage or industrial shop because it was left idle until after the nonresidential use ruling had been lifted.

Fred and Marjorie Sharpe bought S.S. 7 Chinguacousy (School Section 7) for $7,500 when it was auctioned off in 1961. Fred had attended the school for eight years and his wife, Marjorie, was a teacher there for a period of time. With no real need for it, they did little with the schoolhouse and yard except maintenance. But when their son David inherited the property in the late 1980s, and his wife, Margaret, fell in love with it, restoration began.

David and Marjorie Sharpe, according to the author of a 1994 *Harrowsmith* article, "live in possibly the most opulent schoolhouse conversion in Ontario." The original 1,200-square-foot classroom is now a dining-living room and still has plenty of space for a pool table. Marjorie admits that some people find this huge open room with cathedral ceilings a bit "cavernous," but she loves it. A 2,500-square-foot addition contributes to the opulence referred to in *Harrowsmith,* as do the new doors and windows that replicate those installed in 1879 when the schoolhouse was built. The original bell was given a new home in an almost perfect replica of the school's cupola, and the maple floors, wainscotting and blackboard were fully restored. All of this is enclosed in locally quarried, cut limestone that has, not surprisingly, stood the test of time.

Although limestone schoolhouses such as the Sharpe's are generally more intricately designed than their redbrick cousins, S.S. 3 Caledon at Silvercreek is an exception. Situated next door to one of the few Catholic churches constructed in Caledon Township, S.S. 3 is further evidence that Silvercreek was once a bustling village. Silvercreek, formerly known as Caldwell, also housed three hotels, a store, grist mill, blacksmith shop and wagon factory. Pam McAlpine (née Neil) attended the Silvercreek school. From 1956 to 1963, for Grade 2 through to Grade 8, Pam walked the short distance between her family's farm and the school on the hill. Although she has fond memories of her first teacher, Helen Flewelling, Pam speculates that her replacement, Mrs. Cook, is long underground. "She looked old when we had her. She wore those black boots and drove in everyday from Belwood, a long way in those days," recalls Pam. In fact, Violet Cook started teaching in 1918 and was still on the platform in 1963 when Silvercreek's twenty-nine students were moved over to the new Caledon Central

Public School. At the time, Violet Cook told the *Toronto Star,* "Mind, I think they're doing the right thing. For example, I have several children who are very bright — one girl in Grade Two in particular — who'll be able to go into accelerated classes in the new school. They'd never be able to do that in a one-room school."

Built in 1884, the Silvercreek schoolhouse reflects the directions prepared by Dr. John George Hodgins, Ontario's deputy minister of education in the 1870s. He wrote a 270-page instruction book on schoolhouse construction. He recommended that they "should have a pleasant location not on the highway, nor be near to noisy factories, distilleries or pork houses, and a safe distance from all sources of malaria." Fortunately for Silvercreek's alumni, their school met all these standards. His decrees continued: Separate boys' and girls' entrances — also a feature of the Silvercreek school — "were needed

This limestone schoolhouse, S.S. 7 Chinguacousy, on Old School Road was renovated by a couple very familiar with the school. His father was a former student and his mother taught in the school before it closed in the early 1960s.

to prevent the possibility of improper communication between boys and girls."

Designated a heritage building in 1985, the Silvercreek schoolhouse was purchased in 1967 by its current owners, Gene and Laura Aliman. According to the Town of Caledon Heritage Resources Officer, Heather Broadbent, "This structure is certainly one of the best preserved and architecturally interesting schoolhouses in the Town of Caledon." Its distinguishing features include its resemblance to church architecture of the same era. It has semicircular window heads, brick buttresses and a decoration in the brickwork that resembles an orb and cross. A bell and bell tower, replaced in 1988, crown this gem.

The Alimans' experience when buying their schoolhouse is evidence of the chasm that fortunately separated the policies of the Township of Caledon from Albion and Chinguacousy with regard to the appropriate use of these buildings. Gene takes pride in the letter his wife composed and included with their sealed tender to the School Board. It described how the Alimans planned to lovingly restore the schoolhouse and live there on a full-time basis. It talked about how important the schoolhouse was to Caledon's heritage and painted a picture of the quiet life the Alimans had in mind for their new home. The Alimans believe that it was for this reason their tender was selected, despite not being the highest bid.

Both the redbrick schoolhouses represented by the Silvercreek school and limestone structures such as the Sharpes' are found with some regularity in Caledon. Less well represented are examples such as Rosehill S.S. 11 Caledon. Its front entrance is on the side instead of the end of the building. This geometry gives it a very different appearance. One has to look twice to be sure it is a renovated schoolhouse. But its ten-foot-high narrow windows

Albert Street Public and Continuation School in Bolton, circa 1918.

and the stately maples that enclose the schoolyard give away the building's past. Students planted those maples in 1897 to mark Queen Victoria's Diamond Jubilee. Built in 1872 of local limestone, the school had as few as fourteen students in 1944 and as many as eighty the year it opened. Twenty-two children were in attendance when it was closed in 1964. The hamlet of Rosehill took its name from the school rather than the other way around. In turn, the school used this moniker because of the lovely rolling hills in the area and the roses that grew along the roadsides. The Rosehill schoolhouse has been a private residence since it was first sold in 1964. Its view to the west looks down over the Forks of the Credit and the site of yet another redbrick schoolhouse.

Whereas Violet Cook, the last teacher to dust the chalkboard at Silvercreek S.S. 3, felt a one-room school held back bright students, the longtime schoolmistress at S.S. 19 Caledon had a different out-look. The sole teacher in charge of Grades 5, 6, 7 and 8, Winnie Longstreet was nicknamed "Windbag" by her mischievous students. She taught at the small redbrick schoolhouse that is hidden away in the Forks of the Credit. During Mrs. Longstreet's tenure, a number of pupils took advantage of sitting shoulder to shoulder with older kids. Elly VanZoelen completed her public schooling in Caledon's one-room schoolhouses, including S.S. 19. When she finished Grade 8, Elly was a mere ten years old, having skipped three grades along the way. She went on to complete a university degree the same year as she turned eighteen.

Another student who attended S.S. 19 for Grades 4 and 5 eventually became a foreign correspondent with the *Globe & Mail.* He demonstrated his writing skills early. In Grade 5, the presence of more senior students seemed to be helping him along. Asked to use the word "odour" in a sentence, this future professional writer came

These students are positioned in front of the Alton Public School, circa 1935. It is the only original redbrick schoolhouse in Caledon where children still attend classes.

up with the following: "The odour that emerged from the enchantress's cave entranced and intrigued the fatigued soldier to his doom." Not bad for a one-room-schoolhouse-educated ten-year old.

S.S. 19 is a simple building that was erected in 1884 on land donated by Kenneth Chisholm, a local quarry owner. Chisholm's memory is kept alive by the street that is named in his honour. His and other quarries in the area were the reason that S.S. 19 had 150 students in 1890. This number dwindled to three in 1950 as the quarrying and other local industries had died out. When S.S. 19 closed in 1963, the pupils were moved to the new four-room schoolhouse in Belfountain and the building was converted into a private residence.

The Silvercreek school is located "a safe distance from all sources of malaria," as required by Ontario's government of the day.

Alton, in the furthest northern reach of Caledon, was also affected by the health of its industries. A strong candidate for the area's most picturesque village, Alton also boasts having the oldest still-operating school in the Town of Caledon. Built as a one-room school, with "an adjoining room," in 1875, it has been renovated and added to on a number of occasions. However, it wasn't until the early 1900s that all the rooms that comprised S.S. 15 Caledon were put under one roof. Its huge front windows are a striking feature of this schoolhouse, but what makes it truly stand out are the one-hundred-plus students that attend Caledon's smallest school.

Some fifteen elementary and three secondary schools have replaced the forty-one schoolhouses that were Caledon's only answer to education until the early 1960s. Mayfield Secondary School was the Town of Caledon's first high school and it didn't open until 1969. Before this date, students had to travel to Erin, Orangeville or Brampton to extend their education past Grade 8. This might sound like a hardship but it pales in comparison to the miles that the grandparents of today's secondary school students covered on horseback, by foot or by train in order to take their lessons. For until the 1960s, crank telephones, spotty electricity and one-room schoolhouses characterized Caledon.

FLYFISHING, FREESTYLE & FORE

When it comes to toys, Chris Haney, co-owner of the Devil's Pulpit Golf Association, is in a different league. Owning a BMW might have a nice ring to it. But Chris says the thing that keeps him off the streets is his $40-million golf facility. Talking about his two courses — the Devil's Pulpit and the Devil's Paintbrush — complete with clubhouses, pro-shops and more, Chris says, "It's just a big toy."

Perched three-quarters of the way up Caledon Mountain, on the east side of Highway 10, the Devil's Pulpit course commands some of the finest views in Caledon. Teeing off for the first tee, the Tower Tee, golfers can gaze down the shaft of their golf club across the Peel Plain all the way to Toronto's CN Tower. The seventh, the Devil's Pulpit Tee, looks out over the hump-backed Niagara Escarpment where the Credit River has carved out a well-known steep cliff that is known by this name. Golfers are faced with one of three greens after teeing off from the eleventh tee, the Horseshoe Tee. This one remembers the nearby Horseshoe Curve of the old Toronto, Grey & Bruce Railway where, in 1907, a train bound for the Toronto Exhibition flew the tracks, killing 7 and injuring 144.

Chris's decision to build a golf course came about in a Bolton pub in 1985. When he complained about his trouble getting a tee time, an acquaintance asked him why he didn't just build his own golf course. Though it would be a laughable idea for most of us,

Chris, whose prospects changed a whole bunch after he and his partner Scott Abbott began marketing their Trivial Pursuit game, took up the challenge.

Telling himself he had to find a site for the course that had views and was within the boundaries of Highways 400, 9 and 10 and King Street, Chris came across the Booth property. Within minutes he knew he'd found his spot. But acquiring the land wasn't a simple matter, nor was getting approval to build his course.

George Booth and his sister owned the 162-hectare parcel of land Chris wanted. Putting together a deal that suited everyone

The ninth hole at the Devil's Pulpit Golf Course is called Patterson's Grief in memory of a Silvercreek family who lost three children in an 1861 diphtheria epidemic.

took some creative thinking. Eventually Chris agreed to sever about 35 hectares from the lot and leave it for it the Booths. But the $2-million deal was conditional on Chris getting approval to construct — something that took twenty months and $1 million to attain. The Niagara Escarpment Commission (NEC) demanded a complete course and clubhouse design before they would say yea or nay. Over the twenty months, the NEC had Chris change his plans six times.

At the end of the ordeal, Chris got his toy; his course designer, Dr. Michael Hurdzan, became famous; and Ontario slid into one of its worst-ever recessions. The Devil's Pulpit course officially opened on July 1, 1990. Even though a membership in the not-for-profit Devil's Pulpit Golf Association is one hundred percent transferable and the course was rated as the best new course in the country by *Golf Digest Magazine,* it was not enough to pull in very many $55,000 memberships during the early 1990s. In fact, 1997 was the first time that revenues matched expenses.

Today memberships are a more economical $40,000 and members can also choose to play a round of eighteen on the

Custom fly rods are made at the Forks Fly Shop in Inglewood.

Women playing croquet, probably in Bolton, circa 1909.

Devil's Paintbrush. This links-style course is located five kilometres east of the Devil's Pulpit site. Unlike the wide green fairways of the Devil's Pulpit, the Devil's Paintbrush is all hillocks, stone fences and fescue grasses. It is said that while the Pulpit is played through the air, the Paintbrush is played on the ground since there is almost no flat land associated with this course and only the greens are free of the fescue grass.

After playing over 900 courses in North America, Robert Fagan, executive director of the Northern California PGA, said, "The Devil's Pulpit Golf Association is the best thirty-six-hole facility I've ever seen…Winged Foot, Baltusrol, and the rest included." Others apparently either agree or wanted to find out for themselves. Some familiar names grace the Devil Pulpit's guest book: Michael Jordon, Mickey Rooney, Mark O'Meara, Mick Fleetwood, Roger Clemens, Eddie Shack and Dave Steib are just a few of the celebrities who have made the round.

So why is it a not-for-profit organization? Chris says he does it for fun. "This place is run by me... No blue jeans and a collar on your shirt is all we ask. If you want to throw peanuts, go ahead." Chris's casual attitude may surprise those who glance up at the Devil Pulpit's prestigious gates while driving by in a Ford Escort, but it's in keeping with the heavy-smoking, let's-have-a-good-time character of the guy who owns the place. It may seem glamorous to have your own golf course and he probably doesn't have much trouble getting a tee time, but Chris says that in reality, "owning this place and two dollars will get you on the Toronto subway."

Caledon's Forks of the Credit area seems to be a magnet for private sporting clubs. The Devil's Pulpit golf course overlooks the Forks of the Credit and Caledon's most mysterious, members-only facility lies near its heart.

Most people will never see behind the entrance to the Caledon Mountain Trout Club, but if you are ever invited in, take along your cravat and be ready to turn back the clock. The magnificent clubhouse and its surroundings bring to mind F. Scott Fitzgerald

Baited lines are not allowed on the Trout Club's four stocked ponds.

and his wife Zelda — champagne and whites on a lawn-bowling green. When plans were underway to build this edifice in 1902, the new club president, John Ellis, told members, "the Club building will have no equal in Canada. The accommodation is on a large scale, the surroundings are delightful." And for $22,000, the clubhouse was built and officially opened on April 30, 1903, a short two years after the Caledon Mountain Trout Club began.

The property where the club now sits was part of a total of 6,000 hectares of choice Ontario land acquired by the Canada Company in 1844. The 40 hectares that make up most of the Trout Club's present site were sold a number of times before Tom Ford bought them in the 1880s. He built a sawmill, dug a pond and put in a fish hatchery. In 1893, Charles Wilmot purchased the land and facilities and established Wilmot's Trout Preserves. But hard times meant Mr. Wilmot was unable to finance his business, and, together with the land, it was turned over to the Caledon Mountain Trout Company Ltd. in 1901. Its charter stated that the purpose of the new company was "to propogate [sic] and preserve fish and game for sporting and commercial purposes and to maintain a fishing and shooting club and in connection therewith to promote and encourage lawful and athletic exercises."

Local members as well as those from Toronto, Hamilton and the United States used the facilities during its earliest years. If coming from a distance they took the train to Inglewood and then paid the fifty-cent charge to go by horse and wagon to the club. Once they'd arrived they were welcome to stay for a day or a week or more and catch their ten-pound daily limit.

Over the years, ponds were dug and repaired, drained and dredged, but the clubhouse remained largely unchanged until 1918 when a fire burned its annex to the ground. It cost $7,500 to replace

The clubhouse at the Caledon Mountain Trout Club, completed in 1903, was to "have no equal in Canada."

the annex, but a year later the club had new lodgings for bachelors and a fashionable ballroom. The new space was immediately put to good use as dances became a club tradition that continued until 1953 when the replacement annex had to be dismantled.

Fire struck again in 1952. And to her surprise, just as the club's manager, Miss Neilson, was in the clubhouse organizing dinner for the members and guests who had helped extinguish the blaze, she heard a radio announcer tell listeners that the clubhouse had burned to the ground. In reality, the fire caused $5,400 in damage to a locker room that was soon repaired.

Today, not much has changed. The Caledon Mountain Trout Club consists of the Forks of the Credit site where the clubhouse overlooks four trout-stocked ponds containing in excess of 12,000 fish. It also continues to own a fish hatchery in nearby Hillsburgh at the headwaters of the West Credit River. The main pastime for the clubs' fewer than 200 members is flyfishing. No baited lines are allowed. Members and their guests can take their meals in the club's rustic dining room, rest by a crackling fire on a cool spring or fall evening, and as many as forty people can stay the night in traditional bedrooms. Closed during the winter months, the Caledon Mountain Trout Club clings to its historic splendour and, though not visible from the road, it is a Caledon landmark.

Less mystical but no less a part of what makes Caledon magical is the Caledon Ski Club. As seen today, the ski club is an efficient, well-oiled machine consisting of twenty-two ski trails, four triple chair lifts, a quad, a T-bar, two small surface lifts, two lodges, a nursery, two residential developments with a total of forty-four units and probably the most efficient snowmaking system of any private ski club in Southern Ontario. With nearly 3,000 members, it employs 175 full- and part-time winter staff. But the Caledon Ski Club wasn't always such a slick operation.

The Ski Club's humble birth is recorded by Oakland Ross in *Caledon Ski Club: The First Forty Years:*

"One afternoon, in the fall of 1958, Helen Wortley stood with her husband, Ross, by the manure pile that spilled down the western side of the barn. They both gazed across the hollow and up to the west, where a broad slope freckled by crab apple trees and thorn scrub rose above them. Eventually, Helen uttered these fateful words: 'Why don't you put up a rope tow on that hill?'

"Ross pondered the suggestion for a few moments and then nodded. 'Yeah,' he said. 'That's a good idea.'

"And so he did.

"But not right away. The Caledon Ski Club may have been rustic and unpretentious in its origins — a barn, a manure pile, a hill, a quantity of rope — but it nonetheless required some organization and outside help before it could accommodate skiers."

The earliest site of the Caledon Ski Club — home of the manure pile and the hill — was Ross and Helen Wortley's rented farm at the base of the Niagara Escarpment near the "graffiti trestle bridge." Built on Helen's skiing skills, Ross's infectious tenacity and the largesse of its earliest directors, the Caledon Ski Club was soon attracting skiers from Caledon, Toronto and Oakville. But as the number of skiers increased and their abilities improved, a more challenging venue was required. The fact that the club existed on rented land was also not lost on its members and directors.

Opened in 1958, the Caledon Ski Club is a haven for families who enjoy fresh air and exercise.

In return for purchasing ten-year memberships, some seventeen families helped Ross Wortley buy the land above Brimstone and the Forks of the Credit, home of the present-day club. Many of the Club's hills bear the names of these earliest members — Knight's Flight for Bud Knight, Kendall's Kandihar for Douglas Kendall, O.K. Ross Run for Okey Ross, Soules' Skyway for Bill Soules. With a rope tow, a couple of narrow trails, a baby run and a prefab hut, the new ski club began operating in 1962. Yet it wasn't until 1966 that the Caledon Ski Club Ltd. was established under the Corporations Act of Ontario and Ross Wortley was uprooted from his role as sole owner and catalyst to general manager, president and catalyst.

Since those early days, the Caledon Ski Club has had a few downs, but mostly ups along the way. Good snow years were followed by poor ones, and fire totally destroyed one of its lodges in 1980. The club has produced some very successful skiers and ski racers over the years and it has also provided — and continues to provide — an excellent recreational experience for its family members. Furthermore, its runs have been graced by some very famous racers including Jean-Claude Killy, Ken Read and Steve Podborski. One of Canada's most successful downhill racers, Laurie Graham, is from nearby Inglewood and she has made more than one appearance at the Caledon Ski Club. Prince Andrew spent a day on the hills, and segments of *The Six Million Dollar Man, My Secret Identity* and *Due South* used the Caledon Ski Club as a backdrop.

These and Caledon's other private and public clubs provide their members, many of whom live locally, with an opportunity to enjoy the scenery, the fresh air and the simple act of getting together with friends. They add to Caledon's social fabric. They provide local employment and encourage recreation.

Gordon Adams, who now lives near Alton, recalls his first brush with a local club. He visited Caledon in the late 1920s: "We stayed overnight in a hotel in Caledon Village. The next morning we drove to the edge of the mountain, put on our skies and skied down the road. When we got to the bottom we asked around and found out that Svend Jepson (father of Helen Wortley) was a skier. So we skied over to his place. There we found Svend and his wife, Ada. They were so glad to see us that they built us a jump and made us ski over it. Afterwards we suggested they start a ski club." And the Jepsons did. In fact, in the 1930s, Svend cut the region's first ski hill, right down the face of the Niagara Escarpment. And though he never became a member of the Caledon Ski Club, Mr. Adams is the oldest surviving member of the Caledon Mountain Trout Club. He likes clubs because of the friendships he's made through them. "Everyone values their friends," he says. And the affection goes both ways. For three years in a row, the Caledon Mountain Trout Club refused to accept Mr. Adam's resignation. Then in 1998, the club decided to make him its first-ever honorary member. And that is what clubs are all about.

THE ESCARPMENT & THE MORAINE:
A ROUGH & ROCKY PAST

From the top of the McLaren Castle, it was said, seven counties could be seen with the naked eye. And it's unlikely that many counties contain more stones than Peel, and few townships have a bigger share of rock than Caledon. It's not surprising, then, that Caledon has its share of magnificent stone buildings. But the McLaren Castle was the grandest of them all.

Built over six years, between 1860 and 1866, the McLaren Castle was built of local stone. Its eighteen rooms, including nine bedrooms, made it a very imposing "farm residence." An observation platform surrounded by a heavy stone parapet sat atop the castle's 15-metre-tall stone tower and contributed to the medieval look that made Alexander McLaren's home truly a castle. McLaren was reeve of Caledon Township for eighteen years and warden of Peel County in 1880. His castle housed the Grange Post Office for forty years. Although several generations of McLarens lived in the castle, it was eventually sold in 1937 to a lumber company that used it as a bunkhouse — and harvested all the farm's merchantable hardwood timber. Eventually bought and returned to use as a proper home, sadly, it was destroyed by fire in 1963. A shell of the original building, made into a residence, is all that remains of the castle today.

Local stone was used for countless other homes, churches, schools and mills in Caledon. Additionally, Ontario's Parliament Buildings, Toronto's old City Hall and a number of buildings

Toronto's Old City Hall and Ontario's Parliament Buildings are built of Caledon's rocks. The Credit Forks, circa 1895.

belonging to the University of Toronto have Caledon to thank for their stone. Much of it came from the Forks of the Credit, or the Credit Forks as it was known until 1976. It also heralded from quarries near Inglewood and Terra Cotta. The dolostone, limestone and sandstone that surface in these parts of Caledon attracted hundreds of miners. But rocks also scared many homesteaders away.

In the early 1950s, Thomas Graham, whose ancestors settled in Inglewood, wrote an account of Inglewood's early days. Graham recalls, "It was back-breaking work to clear all this land of the timber and even more so of the stones. This latter part of

This stone wall on Mississauga Road is a designated heritage site.

the early settler's work was well illustrated by the number of stone fences, both along the roadway and between fields, which the writer well remembers, and also by the number of stone piles along the fences and even right in the open fields. I remember counting fourteen stone piles in one field of about fourteen acres in size, just imagine ploughing and cultivating that field, to say nothing of navigating a binder around so many obstructions. The stone fences were laid up without mortar but were held in place by rows of split-cedar shingles at regular intervals, and when these shingles rotted out there was a collapse of part of the fence. Now, while the appearance of a new stone fence is pleasant, the appearance of an old one partly collapsed is the very opposite, and so most of the old stone fences have disappeared, having been

shipped by train to Toronto to help build docks and to form a breakwater along the lake front."

One of Caledon's best-known stone fences borders Mississauga Road at the Grange Sideroad. Built by the Patullo family, it is a designated heritage site. Three-quarters of a metre wide at the base, it tapers until it is less than half a metre across at the top. And just as Thomas Graham described, no mortar was used in this fence, but it continues to be supported by hundreds of cedar shingles.

Caledon's rocky terrain soon caught the attention of prospectors in search of mineral reserves. But what they thought had been found in Caledon was the richest mineral of them all. For it was gold that lured many people to Upper Canada's outback in 1818. No reserves, in fact, not even a glitter of gold was ever found, but industrialists noted Caledon's limestone cliffs and they were soon being mined. When the railway arrived in 1879, quarrying really took off. At its height, during the 1880s and 1890s, some 400 men worked in the quarries around the Credit Forks. Labourers lived in Brimstone, while stonecutters and other skilled tradesmen resided in Belfountain. In her book *Place Names of Peel: Past and Present,* Pauline Roulston claims that Brimstone was so named by "the religious and more temperate local residents" because of the rowdy behaviour of the quarrymen that lived there during this period. But whatever the source of their names, Brimstone and the Forks of the Credit were busy places. There were seven quarries at one time and many were made up of multiple mines.

According to the description in Berniece Trimble's *Caves, Castles and Quarries,* Quarry 1 was located a mile below the fork in the Credit River on the Second Line. Quarry 2 was just east of Quarry 3, which, in turn, was known as York's Quarry and was situated on the Third Line, south of the Forks of the Credit Road. It

Queenston shales outcrop in the badlands — the claybanks near Inglewood.

"ran under the mountain for a long way." Quarry 4, the Crow's Nest, consisted of three mines along the old road that followed the Credit River from Belfountain to the hairpin turn. The four mines comprising Quarry 5 ran along both sides of the Forks of Credit Road and were just north of Quarry 4. Quarry 6 was perched above the old train station and at one time was joined by a tunnel to Quarry 5. Finally, Quarry 7, the Big Hill Quarry, sat up high on Brimstone's eastern shoulder.

The Big Hill Quarry used a steam-operated aerial tramway to get its huge eight-to nine-tonne blocks of stone to waiting railway cars. A two-inch steel cable crossed the valley, carrying these mighty rocks overhead. On the south side of the river, rail sidings were extended to the base of the Escarpment's cliffs. Stones were lowered down to waiting railcars by way of a gravity-powered tramway. The

The Credit Forks trestle circa 1910. The scene looks very different today, partly because there are many fewer trees.

weight of a loaded cart would carry the empty cart back up the hill. A spur rail-line that wound its way up the valley from the hairpin turn toward Belfountain served the quarries in this area.

Evidence of this quarrying can still be seen. Remnants of cables and rails remain, as do piles of unused rock. If one knows where to look, the ruins of an old lime kiln can be found. A quarry pond now used by the Caledon Ski Club was once part of the successful Credit Forks Tile & Brick Company. Parts of an old dam upstream from the railway trestle are left over from a power plant that was constructed to supply a china plate manufacturer. But the factory was never built because local clay turned out to be of unsatisfactory quality.

Another measure of the area's rockiness is the fact that a group of early settlers called their new home Rockside. They became known as the Rockside Pioneers. John MacDonald and his group of Scottish friends and family homesteaded around Olde Base Line and Shaw's Creek Road. The Commissioner of Crown Lands in York duped these pioneers into selecting property at the far reaches of surveyed land. It was only after they'd passed through less distant and less rocky townships that the Rockside Pioneers recognized the trickery. Nonetheless, in 1820, they arrived at their new and very stony home — a result of the fact that limestone and dolostone rise to the surface throughout this area. The magnificent house and stone barn built by John Kirkwood on the land first claimed by John MacDonald is a testament to Rockside's most abundant resource. This farm, the longtime home of Major Charles and Chris Kindersley, is located at the corner of Olde Base Line and Winston Churchill Boulevard. As the millennium ends, this original home of the Rockside Pioneers is the object of a battle between residents and an aggregate producer intent on turning it into a dolostone quarry.

A little south of Rockside, the village of Terra Cotta hugs the Credit River. Its history is also closely tied to its mineral resources. As in the Credit Forks, dolostone and limestone surface near Terra Cotta. The Union Presbyterian Church and the "Fifth Line" schoolhouse on Terra Cotta's south side were both made from local limestone. History books claim that Terra Cotta's quarries supplied all the stone for Toronto's old City Hall, the Timothy Eaton Memorial Church, the Parliament Buildings, Hart House, the Soldier's Tower and Union Station's pillars. In all probability, however, stone from Terra Cotta, Inglewood and the Credit Forks was used for these structures.

While Terra Cotta's quarries were hard at it from the mid-1800s until the 1930s, local brick factories didn't start up until after the turn of the century. In 1903 the Terra Cotta Press Brick Co. opened its doors and in 1911 the Halton Brick Co. was formed. They took advantage of the outcropping of red Queenston shale that appears in this area. The badlands, claybanks near Inglewood,

Built between 1860 and 1866, the McLaren Castle really was a castle.

are Caledon's best-loved example of this formation. They also account for Terra Cotta's name, which means baked clay.

The brickyards along Mississauga Road are a well-known landmark. Now owned by Brampton Brick Ltd., these old buildings have a colourful past. The first bricks came off the press of the Interprovincial Brick Company in 1914. Carmen Delutis, who joined the company in 1922 and continued working there until he retired forty years later, says that during the Second World War he was in charge of as many as twenty-five German prisoners of war. "They got paid — not full scale. They were good workers and we never thought they would try to escape," he recalls.

At one point, the Interprovincial Brick Company was producing 90,000 bricks a day from its six downdraft kilns and one continuous burning kiln. The Westminster Hospital in London, Ontario, and the Skyline Hotel in Toronto were constructed from Interprovincial's bricks. It was taken over by Domtar Inc. in 1928,

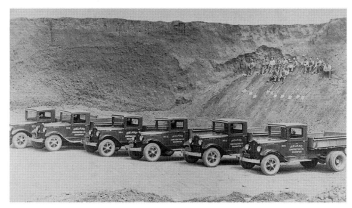

Construction of Winston Churchill Boulevard near Terra Cotta was slow business. Circa 1930.

and the kilns operated until 1964 when the pressed-brick process could no longer compete with wire-cut bricks.

The land and buildings at the brickyards were eventually purchased by Chinguacousy Township in 1972. The Town of Caledon then took them over after the 1974 amalgamation. By this time, a park had been planned for the area and a railway turnstile had been moved there from Elora so that a steam train could use the park and the old Hamilton & Northwestern rail line that traversed it. In 1975, however, the Town sold the land to the Ontario Ministry of Natural Resources to help offset the cost of building its municipal offices in Caledon East.

This transfer of ownership caused many problems. In 1977, the Town of Caledon successfully blocked provincial plans to demolish the old buildings on the site. Unable to knock them down, the province decided to develop the brickyards. A company's plan to build a $30-million brick-making plant was selected. But Cheltenham residents fought this application until, after a long, drawn-out fight, the firm finally gave up. But the citizens' victory was short-lived. They were shocked when the company came back with a new application. This time it succeeded in obtaining a license to remove some of the 35 million tonnes of red clay that lies under the property. For this reason, instead of being a park and terminal for the Credit Valley Steam Train, the old brickyards are attached to a mining operation.

To obtain its license, the company agreed to preserve the historic buildings, protect environmentally sensitive areas and rehabilitate the quarries. The company has lived up to its commitment, but nonetheless, many of the buildings bear the scars of abuse. The province was so out of touch with the historical importance of this landmark that the Town had to save it on yet another occasion.

This Cheltenham home was built in about 1864 of Caledon limestone.

A crew filming *The Wars,* a movie based on the Timothy Findley novel, had obtained permission to shoot some war scenes in the brickyards. It applied for permission from the province to blow up its sets on site. In their wisdom, however, government officials suggested that the existing buildings be blown up instead! It took a Town of Caledon stop work order and a dispute over disposal of the rubble to avoid this tragedy.

The Depression, greater use of concrete, and improved transportation eventually diminished the need for Caledon's brickworks and quarries, but the legacies of these operations live on. Just as mills and houses made of local limestone impress those who see them, many local and distant buildings that were constructed of Terra Cotta brick continue to grace the landscape.

Caledon can attribute its stones, gravel, sand and silt to glaciers that passed through the region on a number of occasions. One result of glaciation that took place about 15,000 years ago is the Oak Ridges Moraine. It dominates the landscapes of Caledon East and Palgrave and is part of a 160-kilometre-long ridge that parallels Lake Ontario between the Trent River and the Niagara Escarpment. The Oak Ridges Moraine is an interlobate moraine because it was laid down in a trough between two lobes of receding glaciers. Sands, silts and gravel were deposited in this trough. After the glaciers had disappeared, a ridge — the Oak Ridges Moraine — remained. The glacial material that makes up the moraine reduces the agricultural value of this land. Consequently, trees have been allowed to return to many parts of the Oak Ridges Moraine and it continues to perform its tasks of air and water purification. Sadly, however, residential development and aggregate extraction are ever-greater threats to this magnificent landform. (The Oak Ridges Moraine is described in more detail at page 74.)

Caledon's rich deposits of limestone, dolostone and shale come from the Niagara Escarpment. This cuesta, or ridge, runs from Terra Cotta through Cheltenham, Inglewood, the Forks of the Credit, Belfountain and Cataract. Then it turns east, passing between Caledon Village and Caledon East before arriving in Mono Mills. The entire Escarpment extends for 725 kilometres between Queenston near Niagara Falls and Tobermory on the Bruce Peninsula. In some places, such as Caledon Village, it is completely buried under sand, gravel and soil. This accounts for the aggregate extraction operations near Caledon Village. But where it is exposed, as in the Forks of the Credit, the Escarpment is spectacular. From the bottom up, its cliffs in the Forks of the Credit around the Devil's Pulpit consist of Queenston shale, Whirlpool sandstone, Manitoulin dolostone, and Cabot Head shale with a very hard Amabel Formation cap. It rises over 100 metres above the valley.

This lovely home near Silvercreek is a fine example of local brick construction.

Its creation began 450 million years ago, at a time when North America was still forming and much of what became Canada was covered by a tropical sea. As described in *The Niagara Escarpment* by Pat and Rosemarie Keough, "Loose materials were compressed, squeezed dry, and chemically transformed into rock: the mud and silt into shale, the sand into sandstone, and the shells, corals, exoskeletons, and lime mud into limestone." Over time, erosion of these deposits formed the cliffs now known as the Escarpment. Its limestone and dolostone and the sand and gravel that often overlay it have long been the target of aggregate producers. But while many pits and quarry operations continue to chip away at the Escarpment, it is a World Biosphere Reserve as recognized by UNESCO (the United Nations Educational, Scientific and Cultural Organization) and much of it is protected by the Niagara Escarpment Plan.

Over the years, those residents lucky enough to live on or near the Niagara Escarpment have battled with the agency that administers this plan. The Niagara Escarpment Commission (NEC) was set up amid great controversy. At one point an effigy of then Premier Bill Davis was burned at the stake to protest against the NEC. A number of commission members received shotgun shells in the mail and on one occasion they were visited in a washroom by knife-wielding property-owners. Several times they had their cars filled with manure and their tires slashed. All this came about in opposition to the NEC's ability to infringe on private property rights by telling landowners what they could and could not do with their land. And though it has made mistakes since it was formed in 1973, the NEC and the plan it administers are the reasons that large portions of the Escarpment have been protected.

Ideas about the Niagara Escarpment, the Oak Ridges Moraine and their associated mineral resources have changed since Caledon was first settled by Europeans. Once they were seen either as impediments to transportation or as money waiting to be made. Little thought was given to their ecological and aesthetic value. Today, agencies such as the Coalition on the Niagara Escarpment, the Save the Oak Ridges Moraine Coalition, Credit Valley Conservation, the Metropolitan Toronto & Region Conservation Authority and the NEC are shedding light on the importance of these landforms and the flora and fauna they support. If you question the need to protect them, try to imagine chainsaws at work on the Devil's Pulpit or earthmovers eating away at the Ridges.

MORE THAN ONE KIND OF SPIRIT
HAUNTED CALEDON'S INNS

Hotels and inns once dominated Caledon's towns and villages. Frequented by travellers as well as the local populace, these establishments were centres of activity. News from away came from visitors stopping overnight in a hotel or waiting for a train connection in a pub. But as transportation evolved and the market for natural resources such as limestone dried up, the demand for hotels and restaurants diminished. Eventually the tradition of a local inn died out altogether. While several hotels and restaurants have taken up residence in some of the lovely old buildings that survived fire and flood, it's amazing how few of Caledon's original inns or pubs continue to ply the trade today.

The Cataract Inn, a small hotel and restaurant, is a survivor. Built before 1870, it pre-dates the 1879 arrival of the railway in Cataract. Industrial development in the 1860s and 1870s was such that the village didn't need the railway to warrant a hotel. But soon after Cataract became the junction of Credit Valley Railway's mainline to Orangeville and its branch line to Elora, it was able to support two inns as well as two boarding houses. (Cataract's history is described at page 73.)

From 1880 until 1916, the inn in Cataract was owned and operated by Mrs. William Glen. By all accounts, it was a rowdy place indeed while under her proprietorship. Mrs. Glen's tenure took in the peak industrial period in Cataract's past, and throughout this epoch there was a steady stream of workers from local quarries and mills ready to quench their thirst at Mrs. Glen's Dewdrop Inn. And many passengers from the eight trains (four on each line) that passed through Cataract each day elected to pass their time in the village's bars.

When Cataract's boom slowed, Mrs. Glen sold her inn to Mary and Kate McEnaney. The sisters were members of a prominent Cataract family and they immediately turned the Dewdrop's bar into a store and the dining room into the post office. It wasn't that the McEnaneys were teetotalers, it was just that the family already owned the village's other hotel, the Junction House.

The McEnaney sisters, along with their bachelor cousins, Peter and Patrick McEnaney, operated the store at this location for over thirty years. After the sisters' deaths, the property was sold a number of times before coming into the hands of May and Jack Denreyer. In 1957, the Denreyers paid $12,500 for a pretty rundown building and wondered what they'd gotten themselves into. According to May, the roof leaked, the floor was rotten and the furnace blew up the first winter they lived in the place. Yet she maintained the business they'd acquired. It consisted of a lunch counter with three tables, a few grocery shelves and a boarding house. But they discontinued the practice that had supplemented the income of the inn's previous owner. His bootlegging had made the place rather popular, especially given how dry Ontario was in the 1950s.

Eventually, the growing demand for tourist accommodations in Caledon convinced the Denreyers to reconvert their store into an inn. They completed the renovations in 1972. And though they didn't move any walls or replace any doors, the new Horseshoe Inn was now ready to serve lunch and dinner and seven bedrooms awaited guests. Jack took early retirement and the Denreyers were seriously in the inn business. For the next fifteen years, they entertained people from Toronto, Brampton, Orangeville and Caledon.

The Cataract Inn was known as Mrs. Glen's Dewdrop Inn at the turn of the century. Frequented by quarrymen, it was a rowdy place indeed.

Most of their dinner guests arrived carrying small brown bags, as the Horseshoe Inn was not licensed. The Denreyer's practice of allowing their clientele to bring their own wine was popular and something authorities conveniently overlooked.

So the day May and Jack sold the inn was a sad one for their loyal customers, some of whom booked every year — a full year in advance — to make certain they'd get their favourite room and table during the autumn season. More than ten years later, May still misses the inn and wonders if she should have sold it. But she says the next owner worked hard to get her to part with her inn. For two years, Rodney Hough came by regularly to ask May when she was going to sell. Finally in 1987, a deal was done and the Denreyers gave up the baby they'd cared for for thirty years.

The first thing Rodney did was renovate his landmark purchase and rename it the Cataract Inn. Chef Roger Genoe and host Robert McReynolds soon joined him. Rodney boasts that the threesome made a formidable team and for ten years they built up the inn's popularity. Now, as the year 2000 approaches, the Cataract Inn has been entrusted to the sole care of Robert McReynolds, who intends to keep a good thing going. Robert recognizes that his inn has a pretty good track record. He also knows that Caledon is a pretty good place to do business.

Another relic from the past is the Caledon Inn in Caledon East. It no longer has guestrooms but lunch and dinner are available in its historic restaurant and pub. Josefine and Bradley Carmichael bought the Caledon Inn in 1990. Josefine grew up in Sweden overlooking Hamlet's castle. There, her family ran a large hotel. The pair met in the Caribbean where Bradley, a Canadian, ran a diving operation and Josefine was working on a charter boat. From this romantic beginning the couple made their way to

The Caledon Inn is a well-known landmark on Airport Road.

The Junction House once graced Church's Falls, now Cataract.

Canada and began looking for business opportunities on the West Coast near Victoria. But the Carmichaels found nothing that met their needs until they came across a newspaper ad describing an inn for sale in the hills northwest of Toronto. They'd never heard of Caledon East — or Tarbox Corners, Munsie's Corners or Paisley, as the village was known at various times throughout its history — but its inn fit their bill.

Historical accounts suggest the Carmichael's new property might once have been a drinking establishment or "grog shop." The same accounts are vague about the exact date that the inn was constructed. While experts say the masonry work indicates it was erected in the 1820s, historical maps tell us that it appeared sometime between 1859 and 1877. Records seem to agree that the building originally sat on a 200-acre parcel of land that was first surveyed around 1820.

But the trail of owners varies from account to account. Some say it was constructed to shelter travellers passing by as they journeyed from Toronto to Lake Huron along the Syndenham Trail, an old military route. But other records don't support this claim.

Since so little about the Caledon Inn's past seems certain, one might as well believe that it is haunted by the ghost of Bridgette O'Shaunessy. Robert and Griffiths Leckey, two brothers who operated the inn briefly in the late 1980s, fostered this tale. Griffiths claimed that supernatural visits were never far apart. According to Leckey's lore, Bridgette, a young maid from Ireland, was knocked up by the son of James McCarty, the man who built and owned the place (and whose name is borne by the Caledon Inn's pub). When James forbade his son to marry her, Bridgette threw herself down the water well and her spirit has been wandering about the inn ever since.

The orientation of the two-and-a-half-storey house, built of Niagara Escarpment limestone, is unusual. Its angled setting on a gentle slope welcomes customers and was probably key to John and Maureen Brown's decision to turn what had been a private residence for almost twenty-five years into an inn and tea house. The Browns purchased the property in 1967, opened up three bedrooms and offered a formal English tea to guests. They also served a roast beef dinner in the dining room and, like the Horseshoe Inn in Cataract, allowed guests to bring brown bags. When the Browns turned management over to the Leckeys in 1988, they still had no liquor license.

It was the Leckeys who opened up the pub and licensed the facility. And it was the pub that saved the Carmichaels while they renovated the dining room and kitchen. For six months Bradley Carmichael chipped away the plaster that covered the inn's lovely stone walls and original beams. And while this work progressed upstairs, the downstairs pub remained open and paid the bills. Today, the James McCarty Pub is a popular spot where locals and visitors drop by to meet friends, quaff a pint, have a bite to eat and possibly encounter a ghost.

Caledon's most prestigious inn is actually housed in an old woollen mill that was spectacularly renovated in the 1970s. In 1881, Ben Ward built what is now the Millcroft Inn in Alton. An expert knitter, Mr. Ward, together with William Algie, rented Graham's woollen mill in Inglewood before Mr. Ward took over the woollen mill in Cataract. He was eventually drawn to Alton when the railway arrived. The tremendous flow in Shaw's Creek

Now a donut shop, the Sutton House Hotel was once a landmark in Caledon Village.

also meant that the water spilling over the mill's dam provided more than enough power for his knitting needs.

Today, while sitting in the lobby of the luxurious Millcroft Inn, it's impossible to picture long rows of knitting machines turning out underwear. But that is indeed what happened in the woollen mill before its transformation. The idea of converting this massive stone structure into a restaurant or inn occurred to more than one dreamer. Paul and Jessie McKenzie, however, were the first to put such a plan into action. They bought Alton's abandoned "upper mill" in 1968. According to a 1973 *Toronto Star* article, Paul "wanted some sort of project the whole family could work on together and which would provide constant company for he and his wife Jessie in later years." The McKenzies worked hard, planning to turn their mill into the Caledon Centre for Arts & Crafts. They never realized this goal but they did open a restaurant. According to at least one Toronto restaurant critic, though, it was not a particularly good eating establishment. *Toronto Life* columnist Jerome Grey wrote in 1977: "I had lunch at McKenzie's Mill a couple of years ago, before Minden's group took it over, and at the time it was quite an awful eating place — primarily, I gathered, for comatose skiers or people who had spent the day looking at autumn leaves and were starving to death." These were hardly encouraging words for the McKenzies, their mill or Caledon's skiers.

In 1975, however, Paul suffered a heart attack and the McKenzies had to give up their dream. This opened the door for the Kendalls. A year earlier, Nicola Richmond (née Kendall) and her twin brothers, Jeremy and David, had had lunch at the McKenzie's Mill. At the time Nicola recalls: "We sat there saying, this place just has to be a country inn; this building is in great shape; all you have to do is put in a few partitions."

The Terra Cotta Inn is yet another fine restaurant in Caledon.

The Kendalls and their partners acted quickly. On April Fool's Day 1975 they closed a deal. For $100,000 plus a $42,000 mortgage the mill was theirs. For the next sixteen months the new owners learned all about red tape. Nicola, who was responsible for marketing, finance, accounting and purchasing, wasn't the first to complain about the requirements of the Niagara Escarpment Commission. She told *The Financial Post,* "You can't remove a dead tree without NEC approval." Suspicious villagers made the inn's new owners agree to plant trees beside the parking area, never play music outdoors and give up any claim to a tavern license.

But $2.5 million and twenty-seven months later, on July 9, 1977, the Millcroft Inn opened its auspicious doors. It had a third-storey addition, forty-two tastefully decorated bedrooms and all the amenities that a luxury inn could offer. But more important, a thirty-nine year old George Minden, famous for his

The Millcroft Inn was built by Ben Ward in 1881. Long woollen underwear rolled off its knitting machines, which were powered by water.

management of Toronto's Windsor Arms Hotel, had not only been persuaded to manage the Millcroft Inn, he'd become a major shareholder. He'd also brought his executive chef from the Three Small Rooms in Toronto.

Later that summer, Jerome Grey of *Toronto Life* revisited Alton. He wrote, "The Millcroft Inn is another triumph for George Minden..." Grey's only regret was that he had waited so long to dine at the inn. An article in Toronto's *Sunday Sun* reported, "George Minden's deft touch is evident throughout. The Millcroft Inn is rural but not rustic. Not a stick of early-Ontario kitsch or a piece of mill machinery is to be seen in the place." The author added, "The Millcroft Inn is a daring adventure."

A year later, almost one hundred years after it was built, the Millcroft Inn received two national awards for heritage preservation.

Then, in 1983, it was honoured by being accepted as a member of the exclusive French Relais et Châteaux hotel chain, which had only 331 member hotels and restaurants in twenty-nine countries. The Millcroft Inn had come a long way from its origin as a woollen mill whose main product was underwear.

Today, the Millcroft Inn is no longer a member of the Relais et Châteaux hotel chain and it's not owned by the Kendalls or George Minden. But the elegance and popularity of Caledon's best-known inn is in no way diminished. Owned and operated by Wolfgang Stichnothe, the Millcroft Inn has been the recipient of a Four Diamond Award for dining and accommodation for eight consecutive years. Its health spa adds a new dimension and it continues to be a destination for people interested in a weekend getaway and businesses requiring conference facilities.

AN ANTIQUE DELIGHT

Many visitors may wait for those crisp autumn days when clear blue skies and the explosion of coloured leaves are reason enough to make a trip to the "hills." But even if the sugar maples, beeches and birches are the main draw, no one leaves Caledon without peeking inside at least one antique store. Recognizing that many people are not dyed-in-the-wool "antiquers," Caledon's shops make antiquing a pleasure for all.

Ann Benitz, who, together with her husband John, oversees Tubtown Gifts & Antiques in Belfountain, says, "Not everyone loves pine furniture. But many men like old tools. In our store there is something for everyone. We make an effort to entertain." Such is part of the secret of the antique store reputed by many to be Caledon's finest. Asked why they have the best stuff, Ann Benitz responds, "Because we like the best stuff." In addition to the Canadiana pine furniture that has either been carefully stripped to expose its natural rich colour, left awash in old stain or covered in thick crackled paint, Tubtown does a healthy business selling Pashmina cashmere wraps from Nepal, dishes from Ireland and candles from everywhere. Though John says the market for architectural details has peaked, the demand for garden paraphernalia is still hot and requests for hunting decoys never seem to end.

The Benitzs' choice of the name Tubtown recognizes an earlier time when Belfountain, or McCurdy's Village as it was known from about 1830 until the mid-1850s, bore this nickname. There are several theories about why the hamlet was dubbed Tubtown. One story is that the moniker came from the prominent placement of the local blacksmith's large octagonal tub. Used to hold the water he needed to cool hot metal, it was located next to the local water pump. But John Trimble says his father had no recollection of hearing about such a tub. (J. R. Trimble founded the blacksmith shop cum gas station in Belfountain that was later operated by his sons John and Roy. Today the former gas station houses a variety of gift and clothing stores.)

History books such as Berniece Trimble's *Belfountain — Caves, Quarries and Castles* give credit to a different source for the name Tubtown. A local resident, Archibald McNaughton, reportedly erected a tub-shaped building closer to the present-day Tubtown Antiques. Made from three-and-one-half-metre-tall staves, it was also three and a half metres in diameter and had a pointed roof. McNaughton used the main floor of his tub-shaped building as a workshop where he made barrels. He lived upstairs. The odd nature of this structure is another possible source of the nickname.

It wasn't until the mid-1850s that the name Belfountain emerged. By one account, it came from the pen of Thomas Jefferson Bush, the hamlet's first postmaster, after whom Bush Street is named. The Tremaine Map of 1857 calls it Bellefountain whereas the J. H. Pope Map of 1877 shows it as Belfountain. It might have been taken from a village of the same name in France, or possibly selected as a tribute to the hamlet's beautiful, water-rich surroundings. At any rate, Belfountain is a popular haunt for weekend daytrippers.

Ann and John Benitz are typical of many of Caledon's entre-preneurs. Not wanting to raise their family in the city, they drew a circle around Toronto that would keep them within about 75 kilo-metres of their main market. When an ad for an antique store in Belfountain appeared in a Toronto newspaper, the Benitzes decid-ed to look into it. That was in 1983, about seventeen years and hundreds of thousands of dollars in merchandise ago. Their shop sits next to their 1860s home — one of the oldest in Belfountain. Now the Benitzes have decided seventeen years is enough. Keen yet sad to be giving up Tubtown Antiques, which is for sale at the time of writing, Ann smiles as she admits, "You have to be careful *not* to make money in this business." This helps explain her confidence that the perfect someone will come along to carry on Tubtown's tra-dition of being the best.

Tubtown Gifts & Antiques may be a popular spot but it's by no means the only act in Belfountain. The better part of a day can easi-ly be spent traipsing around the hamlet, looking through its stores and restaurants. Nonetheless, next on our route is Alton, where shop proprietors have taken advantage of the availability of old churches. Two have become antique stores and one in particular makes a fine location indeed. Formerly home to the Baptists, this church was built

There is something for everyone in Caledon. Here, near Inglewood, an ironmonger builds to order.

from local fieldstone in 1926. The arrival of the Baptists and their associated immersion ceremonies, carried out in Alton's millpond, created quite a stir at the time. A reporter from the *Star* newspaper made the trip to Alton to learn what the local Methodists and Presbyterians thought of the new congregation. One woman told the reporter, "We think this is a sacrilege," and slammed her door in his face. No longer the site of such controversy, it's worth a visit to this antique store if only to experience the open airiness that comes from 30-foot cathedral ceilings and luscious stained-glass windows.

Further down Main Street is the brick Congregational Church. While it lacks the graciousness of its neighbour, it has been the home of Fred's Bargain Centre and, more recently, Fred's Old'en

Days can be spent visiting Caledon's shops. Belfountain is one of the most popular stops for seekers of antiques or other treasures.

67

Day Treasures for almost 20 of its more than 150 years. From his basement workshop, Eric Holmes sells old Canadiana furniture and some antique bric-a-brac, but his real business involves finishing Mennonite pine reproduction chairs and tables, boxes, beds and cupboards. He sells his new *old'en* day treasures to customers from across Canada, the United States and even Europe. Eric proudly tells that one of his rocking chairs was taken to England aboard the Concorde. Since he bought the business from his father-in-law — Fred — traffic through his shop has improved. Nonetheless he still supplements his income in fine country fashion by selling eggs.

Though not much of a store, the Wedo Stripping Centre, also in Alton, is home to yet another tradesman of importance to antique lovers. Bernard Carr, the store's proprietor, makes a living repairing the cane, rush and seagrass seats found in chairs and stools.

Formerly the Stubbs house in Caledon Village, this building is now a shopping plaza.

He is also a professional furniture refinisher and can repair just about anything made from wood.

Caledon Village, perched atop the mountain of the same name, at an altitude of over 425 metres above sea level, is the next stop along Caledon's antique trail. One of the earliest settlement areas, this village ended up taking its name from Caledon Township way back in 1853. Before it was called Caledon, the village went by Raeburn's Corners and then Charleston. The former name recognized Robert Raeburn who, in 1826, built Caledon Village's first house at a spot some six kilometres north of the present location. (Alex Raeburn, who wrote the foreword to this book, is the great-grandson of Robert Raeburn.) The first post office, established in 1839, used the name Charleston and is recognized by Charleston Sideroad, the road that runs east from the village.

In the late 1990s, Caledon Village was a quiet enclave at the intersection of two increasingly busy highways. Several antique shops take advantage of the traffic that rolls through the village either en route to other locales or on its way to discover what the village has to offer. To the true antiquer, the Wooden Bucket, owned and operated by Jean Lynch, is a key reason to visit Caledon Village. The exquisite pieces in her small shop on Highway 10 demonstrate that Jean has "a good eye." Her wonderful examples of Canadiana pine furniture have all been carefully returned to their original wood finish. There are no loose nails or broken hinges on these masterpieces, no chips or gouges, and no cheap orange stain has been used. Each piece is ready to take its elegant place in your home.

Just behind the Wooden Bucket is Tall Stories Antiques. Formerly known as the Clark House, it is one of the oldest buildings in the village. Owned by Dawson and Virginia Ellison, Tall Stories has become known for its Victorian parlour furniture. If

Sadly, Terra Cotta's general store was destroyed by fire.

If you make it up the Sligo Hill you will reach the Inglewood Antique Market. It houses the collections of more than fifteen professional antique dealers, each with a different specialty. One section is completely taken up with architectural details such as old doors. Wooden shutters in every shape, size and colour fill up a wall. Carved wooden brackets, many of them encased in five or six coats of paint, have taken over much of the room's floor space. Old metal furnace grates wait to be made into coffee tables. An inventive mind can come up with dozens of creative ways to use these extraordinary examples of early Canadian workmanship.

In another corner, a bright yellow plastic school ruler announces that Bill Davis is the "Man for the Times." An old fashioned hat, covered in silk flowers, or carnival chalkware figures might be worth picking up to give to your best-friend-who-has-everything on her next birthday. Wooden Pepsi and butter crates, antique books, cat's-eye alleys and more overflow from an

lounging sofas or cranberry chandeliers fit your decor — and even if they don't — Tall Stories Antiques is yet another interesting antique interlude.

After drooling over the Wooden Bucket's orderly perfection and Tall Stories' ornate elegance, antiquers might care to head down Highway 10. Years ago, however, this trip was not a straightforward one. The low, boggy area around the Ken Whillans Conservation Area was once a hazard for vehicles. Rain and snow turned the road into a quagmire, and travellers were forced to detour around the mess. This area was one of several locations used by the Sligo (pronounced *Slago*) post office and was often referred to by this name. The hill at the south end of the valley was known as Sligo Hill, recognizing the difficulty vehicles, usually wagons, had climbing up what was a greasy, twisting ascent. Today, Sligo is more likely to appear on a map closer to the intersection of the Forks of Credit Road and McLaughlin Road, but for a time it was also a name used to denote Inglewood.

Hutchinson's Store in Mono Road, circa 1935.

upstairs room. Antique silverware is the specialty of one dealer while primitive Canadiana pine is sold by another. Jennifer and Peter Willetts, owners of the Inglewood Antique Market, know that because their shop brings together the wares of so many dealers, there is something for every taste. Jennifer says her job is to ensure that all the items for sale are authentic. She also does a good job of making sure there's a treasure here for everyone who ventures through the doors of the Inglewood Antique Market.

Caledon's share of antique repair services continues with the drive down Highway 10. The Lamplighter Shoppe has two proprietors — Susan Hames and Gail Rodgers. As its name indicates, the Lamplighter specializes in antique lamps. Susan looks after the oil variety while Gail is a wizard with those that have been electrified. Being the daughter of John Rodgers, a longtime lamp repairman, meant that her father's former customers were soon dropping off their lamps at Gail's new antique store (a precursor to the Lamplighter Shoppe). This prompted the duo to buy a Sudbury-based enterprise called the Lamplighter Shoppe. Their purchase meant they were able to tap into an already established business and keep John Rodgers' customers happy.

The partners kept the Lamplighter's existing mail-order business going for a number of years and immediately moved the retail operation to their Caledon location in an old honey factory. When asked what possessed Gail to get into the antique lamp business, she replied, "I get a gut instinct on everything I do and it's always right." The Lamplighter's newly renovated showroom proves Gail's claim. So too do the certificates of appreciation that hang on her wall. Both are from Warner Bros. The first thanks the Lamplighter Shoppe for providing light fixtures for the television series *Lonesome Dove*. But it's the second certificate that animates Gail. It congratulates the Lamplighter Shoppe for its antique lamps used when filming *The Unforgiven* in 1991. Gail takes particular pride in her role in helping this Clint Eastwood film win its four Oscars. She also explains how it helped business. Having heard about the role of this local shop in *The Unforgiven's* success, a Toronto television station, CFTO, sent a team up to Caledon to interview Susan and Gail. The clip made the evening news and was replayed on the late-night edition. The next day the shop was packed. Television viewers had seen some of the wonderful antique lamps being sold by the Lamplighter Shoppe and they turned up in droves to check out the merchandise.

Caledon's antique trail doesn't stop here. It could continue across the Peel Plain and end up in Victoria. It could drop down into the valley carved out of the Niagara Escarpment by the Credit River in Terra Cotta. It could double back and take you up on to the Oak Ridges Moraine into Palgrave. And then there are the stops in between. But at the end of the day, it doesn't matter which way you have travel along Caledon's antique trail, for none of them will lead you the wrong way.

THERE IS POWER IN WATER

Hurricane Hazel hit Southern Ontario on October 14, 1954. Over the next thirty-six hours it dumped twenty-eight centimeters of rain, washed out bridges, flooded low-lying areas, swept away homes and killed eighty-one people. Property damage amounted to $25 million. Caledon, particularly the towns and farms along the Humber River watershed, was battered by the storm.

Hurricane Hazel caused one of Bolton's worst-ever floods, but 1954 was by no means the only year the Humber ran over its banks.

By 1900, more than ninety percent of the forest cover in Peel County had been removed. With these vanishing trees went the natural flood control offered by forests. Exploitation of this natural resource caused other problems in addition to the harm to plants and animals, fish and birds. Caledon's mills were also victims of deforestation. Close to one hundred of these factories were built on the Humber River over time. But without tree cover, water levels in the river diminished until mills could no longer operate.

The "forks" at the Forks of the Credit.

By 1948, when the Humber River Conservation Authority was created, the watershed was in bad shape. The Humber Valley Report, published by the fledgling conservation authority later the same year, didn't mince words. It said the river was in serious trouble. "Agricultural soils were eroding due to poor farming practices, rivers were polluted with sewage and industrial wastes, deforestation was threatening headwaters areas, flooding was a continuing threat to life and property, and wildlife was at risk because of the cutting of woodlots and filling of wetlands." It recommended a plan of action that has since been followed and expanded upon by the conservation authority. (The Humber Valley Conservation Authority amalgamated with three other Toronto-area conservation authorities in 1956 to become the Metropolitan Toronto and Region Conservation Authority.)

Even so, pressure on the Humber is greater today than it has ever been. Almost 500,000 people now live within the watershed, and by 2011, there are expected to be 225,000 more. The majority of Caledon's residents live within its boundaries. Their quality of life will depend on how well the recommendations laid out in a more recent study of the watershed — the 1996 Humber Watershed Task Force Report — are carried out. If they are followed, the Humber River watershed could achieve the goal of the task force and become a "vital and healthy ecosystem where [people] live, work and play in harmony with the natural environment." The Humber might also live up to its designation as a Canadian heritage river.

Back when it was still largely unblemished, the river wasn't known as the Humber. It went by the native name Tau-a-hon-ate, the Toronto River, or the St. John's River. The latter name recognized the first European settler to walk the river's banks — St. Jean Baptiste Rousseau. It didn't become the Humber until Sir John Graves Simcoe, Upper Canada's first lieutenant-governor, renamed it after a river by the same name near his Devonshire estate in England.

The Humber River in Bolton flooded regularly. This view circa 1912.

Caledon's other main waterway is the Credit River. Around the turn of the eighteenth century, European traders often gave goods to the Mississauga "on credit" in return for a promise of furs. Each spring, according to *Place Names of Peel: Past and Present,* traders and Indians would meet at the mouth of the Credit River to exchange goods. This practice gave rise to the river's name.

Although its name has not changed since pioneers arrived, its appearance has. As with the Humber, settlement has taken its toll on the Credit. It's hard to picture this waterway as anything but a tranquil stream. But before the Credit's flow was compromised by deforestation, some sixty-two mills had been built along its course, nineteen of them in Caledon. The Credit River was once dubbed "one of the best mill streams in Ontario." In fact, the history of Caledon's towns and villages along the Credit reflects industrial expansion based on access to waterpower rather than development for agriculture. Along the entire length of both the main Credit that rises up near Orangeville and the West Credit with its headwaters near Hillsburgh, the river has been exploited for power.

The Mississauga didn't give up their right to the Credit easily. The first treaty they signed with the government of Upper Canada specified that they maintain the land for one and a half kilometers on either side of the river. In 1818, though, the Mississauga gave up this right and settlers and industrialists moved in.

Later that year lore had it that Caledon was experiencing a small gold rush. This rumour brought William Grant to the upper reaches of the Credit. Once there he didn't find gold, but he discovered treasure of a different nature. Realizing that a stream near the present site of Cataract contained salt, he convinced his employer to finance its exploitation. Together with his boss, Grant

Originally a grist mill, this structure in Cataract was converted into a power plant.

returned to the Cataract site in 1820. He erected a sawmill on the river, built a village of shacks and named this new settlement Gleniffer. However, efforts to mine the salt proved fruitless, as it lay buried too deep for his primitive tools. Gleniffer and the sawmill were soon abandoned and remained that way until the 1850s.

At that time, Richard Church was a land speculator and developer in Cooksville. Since most of the land in southern Peel County had been acquired by then, opportunities were limited. So Church headed north. There he found Gleniffer. He purchased it for $100, and in 1858 he christened his new town Church's Falls and embarked on a plan to establish a self-sufficient community centred around the Credit River. He surveyed 168 residential lots, zoned the river's edge for industrial development, and mapped out a system of streets, each one named after one of his children.

By 1865 he had opened a post office in his store, and had built a sawmill, woollen mill and grist mill. He had also founded a stave and barrel plant, broom factory and brewery — though these three enterprises were short-lived. Although he sold most of his holdings long before he died in 1893, Richard Church was the catalyst that brought industry and, for a period, great prosperity to Cataract.

When the Credit Valley Railway (CVR) arrived in 1879, Church's Falls was asked to change its name to avoid confusion with the town of Churchville. The name Cataract was agreed upon by all except, presumably, Richard Church and his family. The railway brought even more industry to the village. One enterprise was the bottling works of J. J. McLaughlin. To take advantage of the clean, abundant water that flowed from Caledon's hills, McLaughlin erected a bottling works in Cataract in 1911. Its pure aqueous product, known as White Mountain Spring Water and J. J. McLaughlin-Hygeia Waters, was shipped to Toronto by rail in five- and ten-gallon jugs. Tanker trucks eventually eliminated the need for McLaughlin's bottling works, but he continued to draw water from the area until the 1970s. He used this resource from Cataract to make Canada Dry soft drinks since, upon his return to Toronto, McLaughlin founded this legendary company.

The Oak Ridges Moraine and the Niagara Escarpment can be credited for providing Caledon with its pure water. The Oak Ridges Moraine extends for 160 kilometres, from near the Trent River until it collides with the Niagara Escarpment near Cataract. The sand and gravel laid down in this moraine by glacial activity that took place a mere 1,500 years ago naturally cleanses water as it makes its cyclical trip from the Earth's surface down to aquifers, underground waterways, and back to the surface. Hundreds of streams emerge from this moraine, adding to the flow of Caledon's rivers. Characteristic of the Oak Ridges Moraine is the hummocky landscape near Cataract. The kames (moundlike hills) and kettles (depressions that sometimes form lakes) in the Forks of the Credit Provincial Park, as well as the magnificent vistas that roll out forever near Palgrave, are typical of the Oak Ridges Moraine.

The Niagara Escarpment is better known than the Oak Ridges Moraine. UNESCO (the United Nations Education, Scientific and Cultural Organization) officially recognized its dramatic landscape and biological significance by designating it a World Biosphere Reserve in 1990. Made of rock that was laid down some 450 million years ago, this 725-kilometer-long landform traverses Caledon as it stretches between Queenston and Tobermory. Dozens of rivers spring forth from the Niagara Escarpment. Caledon's main waterways, the Humber and the Credit, are no exception. Their headwaters lie just beyond Caledon's northern border.

The Humber River has been designated a Canadian heritage river.

This spring-fed fountain in the Belfountain Conservation Area was recently repaired.

Cataract, which lies at an interface of these two landforms, continues to supply this natural resource. Every day the Crystal Springs Beverage Co. extracts between 136,000 and 227,000 litres of water from its two wells near Cataract. In fact, the company continues to draw water from the same well used by Canada Dry so many years ago. The blue Crystal Springs label is a familiar sight in stores and restaurants throughout Southern Ontario. This pure water is a tribute to the unique geology that makes Caledon so important to the health of the entire Southern Ontario bioregion.

But Cataract's watery history continues. John Deagle arrived in Cataract in 1885 after combing the countryside in pursuit of a new grist mill. He'd bicycled over 1,600 kilometres of Southern Ontario before arriving in Caledon. Here he found a robust river unlike his former mill site near Brantford where water flow had dwindled. He also found a burned-out grist mill, since it had been badly damaged

by fire earlier in the year. Nonetheless, Deagle bought it for $1,800 and proceeded to rebuild until the mill was five storeys tall. But Deagle had difficulty competing with the myriad of other mills in the area. Luckily, his electrical know-how saved the day. Soon he'd abandoned his grinding stones and was using the Credit River to produce electricity. His first project brought lights to Cataract's streets. Then, on November 2, 1899, Deagle's electrical lines arrived in Erin, lighting the William Laughlin farm — the first electrically lit farm in Ontario — along the way.

In 1905, Deagle put up a new sign, The Cataract Electric Co. Ltd., and by 1906 he'd reinforced the dam and reservoir and made dramatic improvements to the generating station. He was also sending electricity all the way to Alton and Orangeville. With his newfound wealth, Deagle undertook an ambitious scheme that would have increased his generating capacity considerably, had it ever been completed. Before the horrendous floods of 1912, he had already constructed about half the length of a 215-metre tunnel. It was intended to carry water from the Cataract reservoir down to Brimstone, a drop of 51 metres (versus the 21-metre head of the Cataract falls). However, the April 6 and 7 flood in 1912 killed Deagle's plans. Extensive damage to his facilities meant he had to apply all of his resources to rebuilding his dam and penstocks.

The Dominion Street road and bridge were also washed away by the flood. But unlike the plant they were never rebuilt. Today, there is no direct road access between Brimstone and Cataract. There is, however, an unfinished, concrete-reinforced tunnel buried under Caledon's hills.

By 1915, when Deagle sold his company, deforestation had started to take its toll and the water level in the Credit through Cataract was declining. The average flow in 1915 was less than one one-hundredth of what Deagle had once seen during spring runoff. The facility changed hands several times in the ensuing years. In 1925 the Caledon Electric Company was formed. Under this guise, diesel generators were added to supplement water power. By the time Ontario Hydro purchased the facility in 1944, more than fifty percent of its power was being produced thermally. The plant remained in operation until 1947. Afterwards, plans to turn the Cataract reservoir into a tourist attraction were thwarted by Canadian Pacific Railway, and in 1953 the dam was blown up and Cataract lost its precious lake. Today, Bruce Trail hikers and other visitors are nonetheless awed by what's left of the mill and its waterfall.

Regardless of all the dams and mills that have been built and destroyed along both the Credit and Humber Rivers and despite runoff from houses, farms, golf courses and roadways, these watercourses have somehow managed to maintain much of their integrity. The two conservation authorities, Credit River Conservation and the Metropolitan Toronto & Region Conservation Authority, often help them along. Today, Caledon contains eighty-eight percent of the woodlands in Peel Region (almost 16,000 hectares). Much of it is included in the Glen Haffy, Belfountain, Terra Cotta and Albion Hills Conservation Areas and in the Bolton Resource Management Tract. Furthermore, where forests appear in Brampton and Mississauga, they are predominantly within the Humber and Credit River valleys.

Development and population growth have also caused Caledon's array of flora and fauna to change. Yet 1990 marked a historic and hopeful event. That year, for the first time in over a century, an Atlantic salmon returned to spawn in the Credit River. Salmon hatcheries are now located in the Belfountain Conservation Area and the Islington Sportsman's Club. Provincially sponsored research programs are investigating ways to improve habitat for salmon in both rivers, and a limited number of adult fish with radio tags have been released. They are providing researchers with feedback on the life cycle of this noble species. In 1998, the Credit River Fisheries Management Plan received the first provincial grant under the Wildlife Protection and Enhancement Fund. The

money is being used to improve conditions for fish, in part because fishing is the most common recreational activity on the river and, more important, because healthy fish are an essential component of a healthy river.

Both the Credit and Humber offer some excellent cold water habitat for Atlantic salmon, brook and brown trout, among others. Though neither river can live up to past accounts that claim salmon were so plentiful they overflowed the banks, fishing in Caledon is improving. This is especially true of the Credit, where strict policies of catch and release mean that fish populations are flourishing. On any early morning during the fishing season, men and women, many with fly rods, can be spied along Caledon's bountiful streams and rivers enjoying the sights and sounds as much as the thrill of a rod bent by the tug of a brook trout.

This kettle lake in Albion is typical of the Oak Ridges Moraine.

OVER THE ESCARPMENT & ON TO
THE TRANS CANADA TRAIL

Canada's baby boomers are reportedly trading in their tennis racquets and downhill skis to pursue less risky sports such as golf and cross-country skiing. By some accounts, birdwatching is the fastest growing recreational activity in North America. As the millennium approaches, Caledon's hiking trails are still more apt to be frequented by those who produced latter-day baby boomers than the baby boomers themselves, but this situation is expected to change over time. Lifestyles are metamorphosing as more and more people elect to spend their leisure time walking through a forest or beside a quiet stream.

When Southern Ontario's hikers decide to hit the trails, there's a good chance they will head for the Bruce Trail. The brainchild of Ray Lowes, the Bruce Trail is a continuous footpath that follows the 725-kilometre-long Niagara Escarpment. Lowes proposed the idea to the Federation of Ontario Naturalists in 1960, and by 1963 the Bruce Trail Association had been incorporated. With funds from the Atkinson Foundation, a full-time trail director, Phil Gosling, was soon hired and development of the trail began.

The opening of the Bruce Trail coincided with Expo '67, the celebration that marked Canada's centennial. On June 10, 1967, the Honourable Rene Brunelle, minister of lands and forests of Ontario, officially opened the trail, even though the Caledon Hills section — the last one to be finished — was not completed until later that month. But despite being a little behind schedule, its planning and construction were in very good hands. While many people worked hard to get the trail built, Phil Gosling and Tom East were key in getting Caledon the spectacular system of trails that it has.

Tom affectionately recalls the events that led to the trail's routing down the Devil's Pulpit (the trail descends a cliff between the Caledon Mountain Estates and the Forks of the Credit). Lack of cooperation from a landowner meant that a link between the top of the Escarpment and the Forks of Credit Road was in jeopardy. But Phil Gosling noticed that maps indicated there was an undeveloped road allowance along what would have been Caledon's Third Line West (Creditview Road). Starting at the Grange Sideroad and using a handheld compass, the duo bushwhacked their way down the Escarpment's cliff. When their straight-line descent ended up on Chisholm Street, they knew they had indeed found a road allowance and the trail could go through despite the landowner's opposition.

Berniece Trimble tells the legend of the Devil's Pulpit in her book, *Belfountain: Caves, Castles and Quarries:* "In far off days, there were two Indian tribes living in the valley, one on the south side and the other on the north side. A third tribe lived just south of the Caledon Mountain. One brave of the south tribe fell in love with and was refused the hand of a maiden from another tribe south of the mountain. He stole her away and took her to his tepee on the edge of the cliff. When her tribesmen followed to give battle, the braves from the south of the mountain were driven back. However, the maiden apparently did not relish her new home, pined away and died.

"The strife angered the Gods, and the God of Lightning was sent to take revenge. This he did by striking the cliff behind the Indian brave's tepee, splitting the rock and leaving it standing so far out from the mainland that no one could reach that portion. The brave starved to death on top of the rock. More punishment came on the two erring tribes. The blow killed all the game on the land and the fish in the river. Starvation, accompanied by disease, wiped out both tribes leaving nothing to show for their stay, except the huge rock which became known as — The Devil's Pulpit."

This is considered one of the most spectacular sections of the Bruce Trail's more than 1,000 kilometres of intertwining paths. A rope and new stairs make the climb quite manageable these days. They mean that more hikers are now able to use the trail — and experience snow and ice inside rock crevices in July. People travelling this route might even be lucky enough to encounter Barry Westhouse, a local historian and avid hiker. Barry is keeping alive the oral histories he learned from the late Roy Trimble. He can recount stories of the old quarries that once operated in the shadow of the Devil's Pulpit.

To go from end to end along the main route, a hiker must cover 782 kilometres. While such an undertaking might appeal to some, most of the 425,000 people who use the Bruce Trail each year are content with a day's or an afternoon's walk. The Caledon Hills section of the Bruce Trail has much to offer the day hiker. It winds its way along the Niagara Escarpment, doubling back on itself so that

Caledon's trails are open year round.

hikers get twice as many opportunities to see Caledon's cliffs and valleys, forests and streams. In addition to the 87-kilometre main trail, the Caledon section boasts kilometre after kilometre of side trails. Many of them make wonderful loops that allow hikers to start and finish at the same spot without having to retrace their footsteps.

Technically, the Caledon Hills Section extends from Cheltenham in the south to Mono Centre in the north. However, the trail actually enters Caledon close to Terra Cotta and leaves near Mono Mills. All local trails in the network are cared for by the volunteer efforts of members of the Caledon Hills Bruce Trail Club. Their work means the path is cleared of fallen trees and branches;

stairs, bridges and stiles are installed and maintained; and new trails are added. This active group also organizes weekly hikes with a special Caledon section end-to-end event each Thanksgiving weekend. So much a part of the local landscape, the Bruce Trail's white (main trail) or blue (side trail) blazes are likely to be found close to any of your favourite spots along the Escarpment.

Before it was built, more than one person probably told Ray Lowes that he and his idea of a 782-kilometre-long footpath were crazy. He was likely branded a dreamer. Ian DesLauriers, formerly the trail director with the Metropolitan Toronto & Region Conservation Authority, has a different take on dreams, however. He says, "If they don't laugh at the dream, it's not big enough." These words seem especially apt for the Trans Canada Trail. When completed, this dream will span an amazing 14,200 kilometres. It will link the Atlantic Ocean to the Pacific and be the longest trail of its kind in the world. Slated for completion on September 9, 2000, the Trans Canada Trail has captured the imagination of thousands of Canadians including many residents of Caledon.

The 33-kilometre Caledon Trailway and the 47-kilometre Elora Cataract Trailway make up part of the route. Furthermore, the pavilion in Caledon East was the first one to be built on the Trans Canada Trail. Opened in 1996, it contains twenty-seven acrylic panels into which the names of donors are etched. Anyone who has hiked, cycled, ridden or skied the Caledon Trailway will know that Caledon East comes close to dividing it in half. The shade of the pavilion and its surrounding park is a perfect place to take a lunch break.

The Caledon Trailway follows the old Hamilton & Northwestern Railway (H&NW) line that arrived in Caledon in 1877. The line was purchased by the Grand Truck in the mid-1880s and became part of the Canadian National Railway empire in 1922. For almost one hundred years, rail service along this route wound its way through Caledon as it travelled from Hamilton to Collingwood. After it was closed to trains, sections such the one that crosses Caledon became part of the trend to turn rails into trails. And it makes a fine route indeed.

Following the trail in reverse, the Caledon Trailway crosses the border into Caledon at Blackhorse. Really a "locality" these days, Blackhorse straddles Caledon's northern border in the far northeast. This hamlet was named for an early nineteenth-century inhabitant who owned a magnificent team of black horses.

Already high on the Oak Ridges Moraine, the route passes through Palgrave, or Buckstown, on its western journey. A pretty village and the former home to David Milne, a well-known Canadian painter, Palgrave is the largest centre in this part of Caledon. Back in the late 1800s, it was the arrival of the H&NW that helped Palgrave grow. And Dennis "Buck" Dolan was one local

Caledon Trailway crosses over this bridge on Duffy's Lane.

resident who probably benefited when the train hit town. Dolan owned a tavern in the community and was an avid buck deer hunter. In fact, his hunting prowess and generosity with his catch resulted in the village being known as Buckstown for many years.

Passing through Caledon East, Cardwell Junction, Inglewood and Cheltenham, the Caledon Trailway eventually arrives at its terminus near Terra Cotta. Some day, before September 9, 2000, it is hoped, this path will be part of an unbroken link from sea to sea, as promised on Canada's coat of arms, "ad mari us que ad mare."

Caledon's contribution to hiking goes on. The Humber Valley Heritage Trail presents yet another opportunity for hikers. It extends for 15 kilometres between the Albion Hills Conservation Area and Bolton. It is the first part of yet another dream that will one day connect the Bruce Trail to Lake Ontario through the Humber River valley.

From the moment the Humber Valley Heritage Trail was first discussed at a September 1994 meeting of the Metropolitan Toronto & Region Conservation Authority, there was no stopping its proponents from realizing their goal. Before Halloween arrived, the team that included Dan O'Reilly, Bill Wilson and others had picked out a route. Early in the new year, a public meeting was hosted and the first chapter of the Humber Valley Heritage Trail Association, the Bolton-Palgrave Chapter, had been formed.

Organizers spent the 1995 hiking season blazing the trail, building bridges and stiles and finding access points. The Boy Scouts helped out and so did the Bolton Horticultural Society. A logo design contest engaged public school students. The trail provided a local artist, Lyndia Terre, who often features local trails in her sketches, with a way of showing her appreciation for the Humber River valley.

At one time these brickworks near Cheltenham produced some 90,000 bricks a day.

The first official hike along the Humber Valley Heritage Trail took place in May 1996, a short eighteen months after the dream was conceived. Although building a hiking trail may not seem like a major undertaking, it's amazing what has to be done before hikers and walkers can get out and enjoy a new route. Marking the trail and providing river and fence-line crossings are the obvious tasks. But the work doesn't stop there. Permission from private citizens owning land along the route must be negotiated; insurance for personal injury has to be purchased; parking areas must be found; signs have to be designed, built and erected; trail maps are drawn and descriptive brochures created. Volunteers are needed to maintain the trail and memberships, and other fundraising campaigns must secure precious cash.

A biological evaluation was also carried out. It helped ensure that the trail's final route avoided environmentally sensitive areas. Man's intrusion into natural landscapes can have deleterious affects on plants and animals, birds and other wildlife. Backers of this trail wanted to ensure their efforts wouldn't do more harm than good. The Humber Valley Heritage Trail's evaluation turned up many interesting facts. A number of regionally rare birds were identified, including the white-throated sparrow (*Zonotrichia albicollis*) and the blue-winged warbler (*Vermivora pinus*). The veery (*Catharus fuscenscens*), the golden-winged warbler (*Vermivora chrysoptera)* and the mourning warbler (*Oporornis philadelphia)* three species that are declining in North America, probably breed in the area, and the sensational scarlet tanager (*Piranga olivacea)* may reproduce along the trail's route. These species of birds, as well as leopard frogs (*Rana pipiens*) and spring peepers (*Hyla crucifer*) are just some of the sights and sounds the Humber Valley Heritage Trail has to offer.

Most people who are familiar with Caledon's trails have a favourite route, a special tree, or a secret location where they know they'll find a showy lady's slipper, a morel or a walking fern. Maybe it's a lookout where they can watch winter burst into spring or summer explode into autumn. A stretch of trail that brings great inner peace or an eddy of a trickling brook where they know fish are apt to while away a lazy afternoon. It may be a steep hill that, once climbed, proves the hiker is still as fit as ever or a favourite route that ends at a local pub or restaurant. Caledon's trails are available to anyone, at any time of the year. They can be hiked or skied and some can be navigated by horses and bicycles. These trails open up Caledon's inner beauty for all to share. In return, the Bruce Trail Association asks that you "leave only your thanks and take nothing but photographs."

THE METHODISTS HAD THEIR APPEAL

It's not uncommon to come across a lovely old church and cemetery sitting all alone on a barren hillside in Caledon. Two Catholic churches — St. John's Albion, just east of Caledon East and St. Cornelius on Kennedy Road — are cases in point. Their placement tells us a great deal about early settlements. They hint at a past not reflected in the present.

Though passersby today might miss it, St. John's Albion is actually situated near the hamlet of Albion. Known by this name since 1907, Albion, or Centreville as it was called before 1907,

St. James Anglican Church in Caledon East, circa 1924.

once had a post office, blacksmith shop and an inn. It was also a flagstop along the nearby Hamilton & Northwestern Railway. Its earlier name reflects the hamlet's location at the centre of the old Albion Township.

The redbrick gothic-style church perched above Albion today is the third Catholic church to be built in the vicinity. Completed in 1902, it replaced a frame structure that had served the community for fifty-one years. Its two-hectare site includes a rectory (added in 1908) and cemetery and was donated by William Dwyer. Dwyer is rumoured to have selected land in Albion in lieu of property at the corner of what is now Toronto's Yonge and Queen Streets. He didn't care for the mud of Toronto. Known in Dwyer's time as the Church of Adolphus, the frame building replaced the first Catholic church in the area. It was a small log building that was erected in 1834 a few kilometres north of Albion in the hamlet of Lockton. This community shows up on historical maps and was reportedly named after the Lock family that settled there. Thomas Hockley built a five-storey grist mill near Lockton in 1857.

It was difficult for early settlers to establish regular religious meetings. While the Constitution Act that created the province of Upper Canada stipulated that one-seventh of the land was to be reserved to support the Protestant clergy, this was interpreted by Lieutenant-Governor Sir John Graves Simcoe to mean the Church

of England. But there were few Anglican clergymen willing to venture to distant places such as Caledon. One exception was Reverend Featherstone Lake Osler. Appointed to Albion in 1837, he did more than preach as he travelled by horse throughout his huge parish.

The Story of Albion describes Featherstone's commitment: "In addition to leading a singing school, and operating a lending library, he taught grown-ups and children to read and write. He pulled teeth, prescribed physic and bled patients." And his wife "started a school for 'young females,' which met regularly in what had started out in life as a cowshed in the woods…There they were instructed by their charming hostess in 'reading, writing and religious principles, housewifery and neatness.'"

Featherstone was replaced in 1843 by his brother Henry Bath Osler. He preached from the house of William Wilson, who resided near Sandhill. Better known as "English" Wilson, he was a staunch supporter of the Church of England. Nonetheless, his son Isaac was instrumental in establishing the Methodists in the area. Isaac became disenchanted with the Church of England because of its sparse representation. Instead he was inspired by the Methodists, whose "circuit" preachers were not only more regular in their appearance, but whose sermons were often highly entertaining and attracted large crowds.

At seventeen, Isaac Wilson became a lay Methodist preacher. He rode from town to town attending and leading services. He also hosted revival meetings in his parent's kitchen. Then, in 1848, neighbours helped him build a log structure that served as the place of worship for local Methodists.

Though Methodist circuit preachers were the most apt to visit Caledon's earliest communities, it wasn't until after 1831 that they could perform marriage ceremonies. Previously this right was reserved for Church of England clergymen, Catholic priests and, where no clergyman resided within eighteen miles, for magistrates, presuming there were any. This limitation reportedly led to many common-law marriages and did little to endear the Church of England to early settlers.

In 1861, Isaac's parents sold a small piece of their land to the trustees of the log church. And so began the Salem Primitive Methodist Church, known today as the Salem United Church. Every

No tomfoolery is allowed at the Laurel Hill Cemetery in Bolton.

The Claude Presbyterian Church is one of Caledon's best-known landmarks.

Built in 1837, the White Church on Mississauga Road is Caledon's oldest.

detail of the construction of this simple brick building was recorded. The stones for the foundation came from local farms. They are noteworthy because the fossils they contain indicate they were formed before the last and possibly before the next-to-last ice age.

Lime from a kiln near Terra Cotta was donated in huge quantities and the excess was sold to pay for mortar. The bricks came from Tullamore and the brick-maker, Henry Brown, and his wife, Ursula, are buried in the Salem Cemetery. Lumber came from Kleinburg and shingles from Huttonville. A Methodist choir from Toronto performed at the Salem Church opening in 1862. The organ was purchased in 1918 for $300 and hydro was installed in 1930. Cemetery plots were laid out in 1901, but the first burial was John Shaw, who died in 1865.

And while Isaac diligently worked on bringing Methodism to this part of Caledon, his brother followed in his father's footsteps.

He helped bring the Anglican church to Caledon East and Bolton. The first Anglican church in the area was built of logs 1843. It was located near the Old St. James Cemetery on the outskirts of Caledon East. A frame structure replaced the log building in 1848. It became known as the Old St. James Church and was sold at auction in the early 1900s to make way for the newly located St. James Anglican Church. Since 1901, this impressive brick church has graced the village of Caledon East. Bricks used to build the church came from the brickyards in Cardwell Junction, while the stone bricks used for the St. James Parish Hall next door came from Caledon East's own Proctor & White Sawmill. The St. James Parish Hall was originally built as a Masonic Temple in 1911. When the Masons built a new hall, St. James Church bought the old one. It was slated for demolition in 1999.

Another lovely Anglican church is St. John's in Mono Mills. Built in 1867, this limestone building is now a private residence.

Octagonal deadhouses are peculiar to Southern Ontario. This one is at the Laurel Hill Cemetery in Bolton.

It was named after an earlier church of the same name located in Mono Township. Mono Mills was once referred to as Market Hill. Michael and John McLaughlin built a grist mill there in the 1820s and it became a busy agricultural centre until the railway passed it by. According to historical lore, Mono Mills failed to attract the train for a several reasons. First, railway officials thought it a bit rough. When checking out the town they apparently witnessed twelve fistfights in progress at one time. Also, citizens of Mono Mills decided to hold out for exorbitant land prices. The railway called their bluff and selected a route that missed the town entirely.

A group of Scottish homesteaders that arrived in Caledon Township in the early 1820s became known as the Rockside Pioneers. Staunch Presbyterians, they settled around Olde Base Line and Shaw's Creek Road and built the White Church (also known as the Melville Church). This building is Caledon's oldest surviving church. Erected in 1837, the White Church stands today on its half-hectare site south of Belfountain.

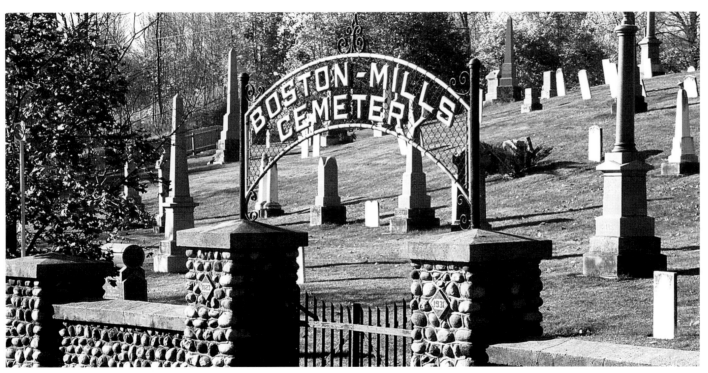

Boston Mills is a small hamlet with a rather large cemetery.

The church has been recognized for its historic importance: "Its simple, clean lines, horizontal wooden siding and delicate gothic windows, though not original, mark it as an example of the unadorned style of architecture popular among many Protestant denominations of that time period." Closed on October 24, 1964, the White Church was purchased by Credit Valley Conservation in 1966. Unfortunately, most of its furnishings were sold, though the altar was subsequently repurchased. Since its closure it has only been used on a few occasions for special services, as in 1971, when Nancy Scott, who grew up next door, took her marriage vows at the altar. Happily, the White Church will soon open its doors once again. The Belfountain Heritage Society is spearheading its restoration. When completed it will be available for weddings, movie sets and meetings.

Though a Presbyterian congregation built the White Church, it

St. John's Anglican Church in Mono Mills was built in 1867. It is now a private residence.

was a United church when it closed. In 1925, the Methodists, Congregationalists and part of the Presbyterian Church in Canada came together and formed the United Church. Presbyterian congregations, unlike the Methodists and Congregationalists, were allowed to vote on whether or not they wanted to join the United Church. The White Church became a United church as a result of this amalgamation even though no vote was ever taken.

Alternatively, Bolton's Caven Presbyterian Church decided against joining the United Church, as did the Claude Presbyterian Church. Located on Highway 10, Claude Presbyterian is one of Caledon's best-known landmarks. Its elegant spire can be seen for miles. One wonders how such a grand church came to be located where it is — in the middle of nowhere. Perhaps surprisingly, Claude was one of Caledon's earliest settlements. But unlike agricultural service towns such as Caledon East or industrial villages like Terra Cotta, Claude had a livelihood that was based on transportation. Highway 10, also Hurontario Street, or Centre Line, as it was sometimes called, was the main route that linked Port Credit to Orangeville and Owen Sound before the railway arrived. A bustling community, known first as Craig's Corners and O'Culloden before becoming Claude, was established to service travellers at the site of today's church. However, when the railway bypassed the hamlet, business dwindled until only the church and a few houses remained.

The 1925 decision regarding conversion to the United Church was a critical event in the Claude Church's history. In January of that year, the congregation voted sixty-eight to fifty-three in favour of amalgamation. Soon thereafter, however, forty-three voters asked that their names be stricken from the rolls. A hearing in Orangeville on October 24, 1925, ruled against amalgamation, but the episode pitted families against one another and wounds were slow to heal.

St. Cornelius Catholic Church is located in Silvercreek.

Built in 1870, the redbrick Claude Presbyterian Church is best known for its spire. Originally clad in pressed metal, the spire was recovered in copper in 1991. During construction, the popularity of this landmark became evident. Scaffolding and other indications of construction caused travellers to stop and ask if the spire was being dismantled. After learning that it was simply being refurbished, several generous travellers made spontaneous donations to assist with the project.

Along with its many churches, Caledon has more than fifty cemeteries. Some of them, the Boston Mills Cemetery for example, are landmarks themselves. Boston Mills is a sleepy community that has not even been granted the rank of "hamlet," yet its proximity to the Credit River meant that it was once the home of a sawmill, carding mill, grist mill, school, post office, distillery, butcher shop, slaughterhouse, store, hotel and power station.

Boston Mills differs from many of Caledon's communities in that it was not named after its mill owner. Instead, it is reported that in the mid-1800s men from the village attended dances in nearby Cheltenham. The last song of the night was usually "The Road to Boston," and soon home became Boston. Then, in 1860, Hiram Castor named his mill Boston Mills.

Although both the Hamilton & Northwestern and the Credit Valley railways picked routes that passed close by, their arrival heralded the beginning of the end for Boston Mills. A short distance away, both rail lines converged in Inglewood and this village became railway central, leaving Boston Mills in its wake. The community also suffered from floods and fires. Its grist mill burned to the ground in 1910, and in 1931 floods took out its dam and power plant. Without a dam, the river reverted to its original course and Boston Mills evolved into a sleepy bedroom community with a rather large cemetery. It is also the original home of The Boston Mills Press, publisher of this and many other fine books.

David Williams, the cemetery's first internee, was one of the first Europeans to be buried anywhere in Caledon. Williams died in 1823, not long after arriving and some years before the Boston Mills Cemetery was opened. He was killed by a falling tree and laid to rest on the hill that is now part of the cemetery. The graveyard's arching gate is also well known. While this iron and stone structure was not added until the 1930s, the original cemetery was marked out in 1858. John Marshall donated the land in return for three grains of wheat that represented the past, the present and the future. The cemetery was enlarged in 1896 and 1908, and in 1919 the cemetery board created "The Perpetual Care of Lots Fund." They raised $1,500 and invested it in Victory Bonds. Today, interest from this fund helps pay to maintain this burial ground.

In 1966, the board purchased the stone schoolhouse that sits above the cemetery and is often mistaken for a church. The Boston Mills Cemetery never had a church associated with it, but the schoolhouse that now serves as a mortuary was the third to be built in the vicinity. The first log structure was erected in 1833 and destroyed by fire in 1853. It was replaced on the opposite side of the road. The existing stone schoolhouse, built in 1888 of local limestone, was closed in 1966.

Another intriguing graveyard is the Laurel Hill Cemetery in Bolton. Active since 1894, it has an octagonal deadhouse and a small rectangular waiting room. According to John I. Rempel, author of *Building in Wood,* "Octagonal deadhouses are unique to Ontario" and are localized in an area just north of Toronto. Until the 1920s this small brick eight-sided building housed corpses during the winter months when burials were not possible. In the public waiting room is a handsome reproduction, hand-lettered sign that spells out the "Rules for Respecting Visitors to the Laurel Hill Cemetery." Originally painted by George Smith, a local artisan well known for his lettering and graining work, it makes it clear that tomfoolery is not permitted in the Laurel Hill Cemetery.

Many cemeteries dot Caledon's hills and valleys. Some are found in unexpected places, such as a small graveyard that is now surrounded by the Devil's Pulpit golf course. In it lie the remains of three children. During a three-week-long diphtheria epidemic in 1861, two related families, the Pattersons and the Harrises of Silvercreek, lost seven children between them. Three Harris children, Leverton (age seven), Emma Ada (age nine) and Charlotte (age fourteen), were buried in what was an open field behind the California Exchange, a pub that was owned by Isaac Harris, father of the children.

This cemetery and many others have been rehabilitated, sometimes by landowners, as in the case of the Devil's Pulpit Golf Association, by the Town of Caledon, or by funds such as the Perpetual Care of Lots Fund in Boston Mills. Headstones, many of which become dislodged or broken, are gathered up and placed in cairns specially designed to protect them from hooligans and from all the wind, rain and sun that Caledon can summon up.

AN EQUINE PARADISE

Despite its rocky terrain, Caledon is horse country. Elegant establishments where carriage horses, Andalusians, hunters or jumpers while away sunny days and wintry nights are neighbours to the signature white plank fences that characterize Thoroughbred farms. Combined eventing — the triathalon of equestrian sports — was once headquartered in Caledon's hills and is still the discipline of choice for many of Caledon's equestrians. On most Saturdays during autumn, the cry of foxhounds accompanies galloping riders sporting red jackets in pursuit of their cunning quarry. And anyone driving down Highway 10 can't fail to notice field upon field of graceful standardbreds grazing quietly, unaware of the spectacle they make.

In earlier years, horses in Caledon were used for transportation. They pulled ploughs on farms and hauled rock from quarries. But during the 1940s and 1950s, the heavy draught animals that performed these arduous tasks were slowly refined through the breeding efforts of local horse lovers more interested in a country hack than ploughing a straight furrow. More equestrians were gradually attracted to Caledon and its equine reputation began to mount.

Connie Smythe, of hockey and aggregate fame, was one of the earliest migrants to find his way to Caledon. Once here he picked up land for a song. He had a nose for a good deal. Smythe owned gravel pits near Caledon Village. He called his enterprise "C. Smythe For Sand Ltd." But he did more in Caledon than open up aggregate

The Caledon Riding & Hunt Club used to host an annual steeplechase.

resources. He set up a 162-hectare Thoroughbred operation just southwest of the village. By doing so he helped pioneer the Canadian tradition of home bred and trained equine stock.

Smythe's record of success is impressive. His Caledon bred and trained horse, Caledon Boy, won the 1958 Queen's Plate. Jammed Lovely, another home-bred, was also the victor of this coveted race in 1967. And her brother, Jammed Lucky, placed second in the same event. As stated in *A History of Peel County,* "It can be safely said that almost every stake race held in Canada

Fox hunting is still a weekly event in Caledon.

and the United States has been won by a horse owned by Conn Smythe." His blue and white colours, a blue maple leaf emblazoned on the jockey's back, also adorned two winners of the Canadian Oaks.

Sadly, nothing remains of Smythe's horse farm. After his death in 1980, the farm was turned over to Ambro Construction Ltd. and became yet another gravel pit. This has left the Smythe equine legacy to the memories of his friends and family and to the history books.

Connie Smythe set up shop in Caledon because of its aggregate resources. But it was his horses that were instrumental in bringing Pete Godson to the region. Pete bought a farm just south of Caledon Village in 1938. He'd come to know Caledon since he was in the construction business and had visited Smythe's operation. When he moved up to Caledon from Toronto, Pete Godson, a founder of the Toronto Hunt, brought his beloved horses with him.

There weren't many pleasure riders in the area when he took up residence on his farm. However, that began to change. Close on Pete Godson's heels came his acquaintance, the colourful Casey O'Gorman. Described by his grandniece as an "irascible, irrepressible Irish rogue, with a taste for whiskey that got him into trouble more than once," O'Gorman teamed up with Godson and other local enthusiasts to lead picnic rides and eventually the Caledon Riding & Hunt Club was created. Founded in 1957, it was set up as a "social club for the encouragement of horsemanship." Still active, the Caledon Riding & Hunt Club was instrumental in bringing the Pony Club and the Eglinton Hunt to Caledon in 1959 and 1963 respectively.

Now named the Eglinton & Caledon Hunt, it is a fixture in the area today. Though condemned by animal rights groups, this most British of British sports continues to take advantage of Caledon's hills, valleys and forests. Each Saturday and Wednesday in the spring and fall, foxhounds come under the control of a Huntsman whose horn signals hounds and riders that the hunt is on and the hounds have "gone away." Or that the day is over and we're "going home." Mounted whipper-ins keep the hounds on track while the Field Master must maintain an orderly field of horses and riders. Formal autumn meets start from a different location each Saturday. As many as sixty horses and riders kick off the day with a traditional Stirrup Cup of sherry, and after the day is done they attend a Hunt Breakfast where steak and kidney pie often graces the menu.

Longtime Caledon resident and Master of Foxhounds until his death at ninety-three in 1993, Major Charles Kindersley wrote about the hunt in 1967. "Due to business commitments the field on week fixtures is often small, however this is more than compensated for by the Saturday turnouts of 50 or more — made up

of both local residents and those vanning horses from the Toronto area. Local Pony Club members can often be seen riding over the country with the best of them and how welcome they are!"

One can only imagine the shocked wonder of city folk who innocently happen upon the hunt when driving down one of Caledon's dusty back roads.

The arrival in Caledon of the foxhunt and of many pleasure riders created a demand for horses and horse trainers. One of Caledon's earliest and most talented horsewomen was Helen Wortley (née Jepson). Helen learned to ride bareback, corralling her father's dairy cattle and helping him tap maple trees in the sugar bush behind their house. That was in the 1940s and Helen and her sisters also rode their horses to the lovely stone schoolhouse on Mississauga Road just south of the Grange Sideroad. Their mounts found shelter in a shed across the road at the White Church.

In the 1950s, as interest in horsemanship grew in Caledon, many came to Helen for horses, for lessons and to watch her special relationship with her equine friends. But demand for lessons quickly outstripped what could be offered even by the energetic Helen. The Caledon Riding & Hunt Club helped fill the gap with weekend lessons for juniors and their parents. Many Caledon riders got their earliest start there under the guidance of Buck Ishoy. Still other local equestrians looked to the Chinguacousy Country Club (now the Caledon Country Club) for lessons where Maureen Brown was a fixture for many years. Her reign was followed by Colonel Michael Gutowski, longtime coach and mentor for most of Caledon's eventers.

Besides these lessons was the Pony Club. Also a British import, the Pony Club was formed in England after the First World War. It taught women and children stable management since the war

Andalusian horses put on a spectacle near Cedar Mills.

meant that stable hands were in short supply. Pony Club camps, the earliest ones held at the farm of Joan and Douglas Kendall, taught children how to groom a horse, muck out its stall, identify conformation faults and generally care for their equine companions. Today, Caledon is home to two branches of the Pony Club — Albion and Caledon — and many young riders continue to learn horsemanship through these organizations.

The Canadian Carriage Classic is a more recent addition to Caledon's equestrian calendar of events. This regal spectacle takes place at Tralee Farm near Mono Mills each July. Owner Dr. George Cormack says his internationally renowned event attracts magnificent carriages from as far away as California and drivers from across the Atlantic. However, local equestrians are some of the most formidable competitors at this annual event. The sight of a gleaming, fully restored carriage being pulled by a pair of identical grey mares is breathtaking. When you realize that the colour

The Canadian Carriage Classic, held at Tralee Farm, is another equine event.

of the bandages donned by these horses matches the livery worn by the driver and groom and that even the quality of the food conveyed in the carriage is judged, you begin to understand the eye for detail needed to compete successfully at Tralee.

Less elegant but more athletic are the jumpers that participate in events such as the Grand Prix. For almost ten years, starting in 1981, the Cheltenham Gold Cup competition, held at Lothlorien Farm, was one of Canada's World Cup qualifiers. At this event, Canadian horses and riders competed against the best from the United States and Europe in order to qualify for the World Cup finals held each year in Sweden. Canada's best-known jumping horse — Big Ben — put in his share of performances at Lothlorien, winning the event in 1986 and 1989. Grand Prix spectators never fail to be thrilled by the courage and athleticism of these jumping horses. Negotiating the immense Grand Prix fences that measure over five feet in both height and width demands precise timing, considerable endurance and incredible trust between horse and rider.

Although Caledon lost its World Cup qualifier when Lothlorien stopped hosting the Cheltenham Gold Cup, the North Caledon Equestrian Park in Palgrave is home to a series of competitions each year. Moreover, this venue has been proposed as a site for equestrian events should Toronto win the bid for the 2008 Summer Olympic Games.

Canada's jumping team has yet to reproduce the excitement of its unexpected gold-medal performance at the 1968 Olympic Games in Mexico City. But breeding programs such as the one at Lothlorien, together with the possibility that Caledon may host the world's equestrians at the 2008 Summer Olympic Games, means that Caledon is doing its part to bring back Canada's winning form.

A winning form is not lacking in Caledon's trotters and pacers. The Armbro name is synonymous with standardbred racing in North America. The twelve orange stables that line Highway 10 display the Armbro logo and hint at the success of this standardbred empire. Taking first place at just about every standardbred track in Canada and the United States and at virtually every one of standardbred racing's major stakes events is the boast of Armstrong Bros.

It started in 1952 when Elgin Armstrong picked up a filly named Helicopter in Florida. A year later, Helicopter won the Hambletonian — the Kentucky Derby for three-year-old trotters. With this win, Elgin and his brother were hooked and so began Armstrong Bros' serious breeding operation. Helicopter produced Armbro Flight in 1963. This filly finished second in the Hambletonian in 1966, and when she retired the same year, she held world-record earnings for a trotting filly ($493,000). Armbro Flight went on to produce Armbro Goal, who continued the legacy by also winning the Hambletonian in 1988. Though no relation to Armbro Flight, Armbro Romance was North America's best three-year-old pacing filly in 1998 and the first mare of any age to break the 1:50 marker over a mile. Not to be outdone, Armstrong Bros' stallions have an impressive track record of their own. Dexter Nukes, for instance, is the second-most prolific producer of offspring that have raced a mile in 1:50 or less.

Whether it's based on the number of champions or length of the dynasty, the dominance of Armstrong Bros' Caledon-bred stock cannot be matched in Thoroughbred racing in Canada. Yet commuters that pass by these equine legends every day are probably unaware of the might of the horse flesh that grazes calmly, almost innocently, along the roadside.

Caledon East is the site of yet another equine legend. Gardiner Farms, with its landmark indoor racetrack, was built by George Gardiner. A stockbroker, breeder of horses, recipient of the Order of Canada, and philanthropist, Mr. Gardiner died in 1997 at the age of eighty. But the highly respected Thoroughbred operation that he built up continues despite the loss of its benefactor. During his lifetime, Mr. Gardiner's horses won over 107 stake races. Sovereign Awards, denoting the broodmare of the year, were given to two of his horses (in 1977 and 1982), and he was the outstanding owner of the year in 1976. In 1992, Mr. Gardiner was presented with the Mint Julep Cup. It is awarded to the individual who has made an outstanding contribution to the breeding industry in Ontario. Furthermore, for a period during the late 1960s and early 1970s, Gardiner Farms was the leading Thoroughbred stable in Canada for seven years in an eight-year timespan (based on race earnings). And one of Gardiner Farm's four standing stallions, Bold Executive, was the leading living sire in Canada in 1998.

Gardiner Farms is a fully integrated Thoroughbred training facility. Its foaling barn, yearling barn, breeding barn and training facilities make it one of Canada's most successful and most prestigious operations and another horse feather in Caledon's equine cap.

In the mid-seventies, Blue Ridge Farm (now Trademark Farm) and the Chinguacousy Country Club (now the Caledon Country Club) teamed up to become the training centre for Canada's Three Day Event Team. Sheila Wilcox, a well-known eventer from England, was enticed to come to Canada to help the team make its Olympic mark. Her tenure proved to be short, but the crusty Ms Wilcox helped bring the Eastern Canadian Three Day Event Championships to Caledon in 1975 and 1977.

A jumper competes at the North Caledon Equestrian Park near Palgrave.

Gardiner Farms near Caledon East.

Though Olympic success continues to elude Canada's Three Day Event team, the legacy of the team's presence in Caledon includes wonderful eventing facilities, some pretty good local eventers and the ability to organize a successful event — something that hap-pens every year at the Caledon Riding & Hunt Club, host of the longest continuously running combined event in Canada.

A different equestrian spectacle can be found in Caledon every weekend from May through September. Endurance riding, dressage shows and even a triathalon that involves riding, fly-fishing and shooting, are interspersed with show jumping, carriage driving, dressage shows and fox hunting. But for a real spectacle, the Andalusians at the Cedar Mills Spanish School are hard to beat. With their long flowing manes and tails, these Spanish horses perform the high school movements made famous by the Lipizzaners — the better-known descendents of the Spanish horse. Andalusians are the gallant breed that took kings to war. Their magical movements are left over from their fighting days. Whether performing the piaffe, the passage or the pirouette, Andalusian horses seem to be lifted along by some giant, invisible threads from the sky. Each movement is sus-pended in slow motion. And just as the experience of sitting atop an Andalusian horse must be a dream of every rider, living in Caledon's equestrian hills must be a wish of all horse lovers.

MORE THAN A MILL FOR EVERY COMMUNITY

A dense forest of magnificent trees greeted settlers arriving in Caledon in the early to mid-1800s. Huge beeches and basswoods, cherry and old-growth pine of unimaginable proportions blanketed the area. Homesteaders battled with these trees, felling them by hand to make way for a field or two where the sun could coax along wheat or a few potatoes. Once cut, trees were either burned as fuel or used to build Caledon's earliest log homes. But trees were soon being harvested for sale. Wood was needed for furniture, boats and plank roads, as well as for houses. The demand for timber meant that sawmills were the first to appear in Caledon. By the late 1820s, water-powered sawmills dotted the countryside. Every community had at least one, if not two, places where settlers could take their felled trees to be sawn into usable lumber.

As more settlers arrived and more land was cleared for agriculture, the demand for grist mills came soon after the sawmills. Grinding wheat by hand was no easy task. The author of *The Story of Albion* captured the importance of a grist mill to early settlers. Esther

Belfountain Conservation Area, circa 1935. At one time there were nineteen mills on Caledon's section of the Credit River.

Heyes wrote, "It took most of the precious evening's hours to produce enough flour for the next day's needs, and the overworked men vowed they would rather chop down trees in the forest all day long than grind one bushel of grain." When a village became home to a grist mill it was quickly transformed into a centre of agricultural activity that attracted other services and tradesmen.

Such was the case for Bolton. In 1823, five years after James Bolton put down stakes along the Humber River, his nephew George opened a grist mill. The small mill had only "one run of stones" but it put Bolton on the map and ensured its future as a bustling, vibrant community. Bolton's grist mill was the first built on the Humber north of Weston.

Lineups at the Bolton mill were common in those early days, but the hospitality of George Bolton reportedly made up for what could be a two-day wait. George's customers were his guests, and he was affectionately known as "Boss Bolton." George's nephew, James, son of James senior, was the miller.

With a grist mill and other amenities, the town of Bolton Mills, later shortened to Bolton, and Albion Township began

making names for themselves — not the least of which came from the local population's staunch backing of William Lyon Mackenzie. So ardent was the senior James Bolton's support for the colourful Mackenzie that he was forced to flee and never return to Canada after the Rebellion of 1837. Albion Township, in those days, made up part of Mackenzie's York riding. And like his other rural constituents, Albion's residents were incensed by the shenanigans of the government of Upper Canada that Mackenzie opposed. After Mackenzie's fourth expulsion from the House of Assembly, a meeting was held in Albion. At that event a series of resolutions, including one written by James Bolton senior, was passed. Bolton proclaimed:

"Sir: We present our grateful thanks for your watchful and energetic fulfillment of the duties devolving upon you as our representative in the Commons House of Assembly — for the manly and honest stand you have so long and so constantly made in defence of our constitutional rights and liberties against the inroads of arbitrary power — against banking monopolies and legalized fraud in every shape — against the corrupting system of favoritism and privalege [sic] — against the system of anti-christ in the form of state churches and state paid priests, which ever did and ever will support those measures which confer all the power, all the learning, all the wealth, yes and all the enjoyments of the goods of life to the control of the few, and consign the multitude whose labor is the source of all those goods and enjoyments, to poverty and ignorance. But above all we thank you for your strenuous and unyielding efforts to extend the means of education to all, especially to the poor and destitute."

In the mid-1840s, after the Bolton mill was destroyed by one of many floods, Boss Bolton sold the business to his nephew, James

Church's Falls, now known as Cataract, was once the site of a grist mill that was converted into a power plant.

Bolton was once a mill town, as depicted on this mural in the town's centre.

The Bolton Mill, seen here around 1960, was owned by James Goodfellow in the 1950s and early 1960s.

"Squire" Bolton. Partly due to the reportedly "monotonous regularity" with which the Humber River ran over its banks, James built a new mill at a more lofty site at the corner of Humberlea Road and King Street. Though construction of the millrace required back-breaking labour, it increased the mill's head from less than one and a half metres to four metres. Together, the extended millrace and the new "three run of stone" significantly increased the mill's capacity.

James Bolton retired a wealthy man after he sold the mill to Edward Lawson in 1854. Lawson subsequently converted the mill into a soda-biscuit factory, added a steam bakery and, after four years, passed the operation along to John Guardhouse. By 1875, Guardhouse was doing half a million dollars' worth of business each year. In 1881, three years after his death, his widow sold the mill to Andrew McFall. While the community of Bolton was named after the founder of the original grist mill, the McFall name was also well known. Not only did Andrew McFall own the grist mill, he also brought electricity to Bolton in 1907. Under the McFall family's tutelage (which ended in 1940), a full roller system, the first one of its kind in Ontario, was installed. A steam plant was added in 1907, and a year later the McFalls invested in a chopper that cut grain for the growing number of cattle being farmed in the area.

As transportation improved, demand for the mill slowly died off until it was closed in the 1960s. Sadly, Bolton's mill, like so many others, was eventually destroyed. In this case, it was intentionally set on fire as part of a drill for local fireman in 1968 and Bolton has since been deprived of a popular and historic landmark.

As the population of Caledon and other parts of Canada grew, local waterpower was put to other uses. By the late 1800s, Caledon had more than its fair share of woollen mills spread out along the banks of its rivers. Knitting machines were quickly added to the carding machines that combed the wool into spirals of loosely rolled fibres that could be spun and then made into clothing. Long wool underwear was a favoured product, but blankets and yarn as well as cloth were also produced in Caledon.

Inglewood has a wonderful old woollen mill. Over 150 years and several incarnations after the first woollen mill was built on

Graham Products in Inglewood still operates in this renovated mill.

task and began carding wool for local women to spin into clothing.

On April 1, 1860, Inglewood's first Graham rented Thomas Corbett's woollen mill. Nine years later the same David Graham married the boss's daughter, Margaret, and in 1871 he took over the business from his ailing father-in-law. That same year the wooden structure burned to the ground. But undeterred, David rebuilt the mill using local fieldstone and renamed the business Riverdale Woollen Mills. A date stone etched with the words "Riverdale Woollen Mills, 1871" can still be viewed on the mill site.

The choice of Riverdale reflects Inglewood's identity crisis. There is speculation that the name Inglewood was the choice of David Graham's daughter-in-law. A great reader, she was thought to have picked it from a book about King Arthur, whose adventures took place in the Forest of Inglewood. Alternately, selection of the name has been credited to Thomas White, the Member of Parliament for Cardwell — the riding in which Inglewood resided at the time.

the site, this lovely stone structure still backs on to the Credit River. It is the only one of Caledon's mills that is still home to industrial activity. Renovated, upgraded and restored, the business bears the name Graham Products Ltd. Though its carding and knitting machines were traded in for plastic pultrusion equipment in the 1950s, and power generated by Ontario Hydro replaced that which could once be coaxed out of the Credit River, the Inglewood mill continues to be a major employer in the area. Even more impressive is the fact that its current president and principal shareholder, Ian Graham, is the great-great-grandson of the first Graham to arrive in Inglewood.

Inglewood's first woollen mill actually pre-dates the village. After arriving in the area in 1841 and having seen a healthy population of sheep, the enterprising Thomas Corbett started building a frame woollen mill and millrace. Five years later he completed his arduous

Overlooking Inglewood, circa 1910.

But its source isn't nearly as confusing as the series of names that preceded it. For Inglewood, from time to time, was also known as Corbett's Mills, Riverdale, Riverdale Junction, Sligo and Sligo Junction. The post office altered the name to prevent confusion with other post offices bearing the same name. Similarly, the village's two railways each gave the junction a different label. By one account, a stranger travelling from Toronto asked to go to Riverdale, was presented with a ticket to Sligo, and told to disembark when the train reached Inglewood.

Although the mill was struck by fire once again in 1903, the walls withstood this inferno and remained intact for the Grahams and their relatives who, except for during the early Depression years (1928–34), kept the mill open until today. And even during the Depression, it provided electricity for homes in the area.

In 1954, rather than lose the family mill, David Graham, father of Ian and great-grandson of the original David Graham, purchased

Two people were killed when a dam gave way in Alton in 1889.

the facility from his grandfather and returned to his family's homestead. With university degrees in engineering and commerce, this younger David researched many options before deciding to enter the reinforced-plastics industry. Although his decision to produce translucent fibreglass panels proved to be a lucrative one, David Graham remembers being almost defeated by the water-powered turbines that supplied his power. "It was almost impossible," he reminisces, "to produce a steady supply of electricity so it was a relief when the water wheel broke and Ontario Hydro had to come to the rescue." In the mid-1980s, just before David's son Ian took over the operation, the mill was completely renovated. Today it is a delight to see and a testament to the stonemasons of an earlier time.

Although Inglewood was a good mill town, Alton was the best. Shaw's Creek, the Alton Branch of the Credit River, passes through the village. It draws water from Caledon Lake and the wetlands that form the Crossview Lakes before running into the main Credit on Alton's east side. So robust was the flow in this creek that Alton's

Alton's devastating flood in 1889.

original survey allowed for nine "mill privileges" — sites where dams could be built. Eight of these sites were eventually developed for sawmills, grist mills and woollen mills.

In the 1880s and with the arrival of the railway, William Algie and Benjamin Ward each built woollen mills in Alton. Both of these stone structures stand today. The Millcroft Inn is housed in a stone woollen mill that was rebuilt by Mr. Ward in 1881. It replaced a frame structure erected by William McClellan in 1845. At this location he carded, spun and knit wool that he ultimately transformed into underwear. He sold his mill in 1892 to John Dods, whose sons sold it to the Toronto Millstock Company before it was eventually abandoned and then resurrected first as Mackenzie's Mill and then as the lovely Millcroft Inn. The more-than-nine-metre head of water that spilled over Mr. Ward's dam is a testament to the power of Shaw's Creek.

Mr. Algie built his woollen mill in Alton after leaving Inglewood, where he had rented Graham's mill. In 1881, he constructed Alton's lower mill and created Beaver Knitting Mills Limited. Along with Mr. Ward he operated a successful business, since waterpower was cheaper than the steam power used by many competing woollen mills. But late in 1889 disaster struck. Ultimately causing $25,000 in damage and two deaths, Alton's worst-ever flood was not a natural disaster. The McClellan Bros dam simply failed at 3:30 in the morning on Wednesday, November 13, 1889. With its collapse, a 5-metre wall of water — all of the contents of McClellan's 3-hectare millpond — descended on Alton. Although the damage was catastrophic, there would have been more deaths if it hadn't been for the strength of the dam at Algie's Beaver Mills. It held for almost 30 minutes, giving villagers time to get out of the path of destruction. Eventually the water tore an

The Algie Mill in Alton is now a studio for artists.

18-metre-long gap in the 2-metre-high embankment that abutted Mr. Algie's dam.

Five dams gave way that day. Homes downstream were swamped. In one, its elderly inhabitants were carried away and drowned by the current. Mr. Algie's was only one of the mills gutted by the flood. Its foundations were weakened and its machinery twisted out of shape. The fact that a 3-tonne boulder was carried some 50 metres gives an idea of the brute force of the water.

A number of the mills never recovered from that 1889 disaster, but Mr. Algie rebuilt his mill, only to have it destroyed by fire in 1908. At the time of the fire, Beaver Knitting Mills employed 60 workers, had a monthly payroll of $1,300 and produced long underwear. But all workers were put out of work on November 6, 1908, when fire broke out in the card room. The fire spread so rapidly, according to an account carried in the Brampton Conservator, that "some of the employees were forced to fly from the building without their coats and hats."

There was no local fire protection in Alton and the fire department from Orangeville had to be called in. With a bucket brigade backed up by villagers, the flames were eventually doused but not until all that was flammable had been lost. The damage to Beaver Knitting Mills far surpassed the insurance it carried and was another setback for Mr. Algie. Yet Alton's "lower mill" was once again repaired and rebuilt. Sold to J. M. Dods in the 1920s, the mill was passed along by his sons to Fred Stubbs in 1935.

Mr. Stubbs retooled the mill and, together with his four sons, reopened it as the Western Rubber Co. June Raeburn, who helped write the Foreword to this book, was married to Fred Stubbs's son Ralph. She smiles as she admits that what kept the mill and the Stubbs family going during the 1940s was rubber...well, rubbers, really. For the Western Rubber Co.'s war effort was to supply Canada's Armed Forces with condoms. The company even received a contract from the U.S. Air Force for rubber prophylactics to protect the tips of torpedoes from dampness. With the end of the Second World War, the market for prophylactics dried up, so to speak, as Canada's baby boom got underway. But, in true pioneer spirit, the Western Rubber Co. adapted to Canada's changing demographics. Soft rubber "cradle" toys, balloons and beach balls as well as rubber gloves were soon rolling off the mill's assembly line. They were quickly being gnawed and chewed upon by the country's growing population.

In 1977, the mill was purchased by June and Ralph Stubbs's daughters, Marilyn and Mary June, and their sibling husbands, Claire and Lyle Cooney. The Cooneys produced balloons and kitchen gloves until 1981, when they sold the operation. After the business moved to the United States, Mary June and Lyle Cooney bought the mill's machinery and moved it to a new location in Hamilton.

Today, parts of Algie's mill have been refurbished. It is home to some of Caledon's most talented artisans. And though they don't use it, the mill's water turbine sits in the mill's basement hoping that maybe someday it will turn once again.

NAMING THOSE LINES & SIDEROADS

In 1982, the lines and sideroads in the northern part of Chinguacousy Township were given names. This process went quite smoothly, so Bert Moore, Director of Public Works for the Town of Caledon, was surprised by the rancour that arose when he started the same process for the rest of Caledon. Bert recalls being visited by more than one irate resident who was willing to come to blows before agreeing to a particular name. Yet Bert was only the messenger. He'd been instructed to apply names to Caledon's roads because of errors made by emergency services. Fire trucks had been known to show up, for example, at the Third Line West rather than the Third Line East. It was decided that road names would alleviate this confusion.

Special public meetings were held to discuss certain names. Petitions were signed when a name was not favoured for a particular road. Things were basically very complicated. Yet by 1993, Caledon's system of lines and sideroads ceased to exist.

Today, old timers cling to their line and concession numbers. And when they do, more recent immigrants are often confused. Over time, the names will likely stick but just as many Canadians have never become completely comfortable with the metric system, some of Caledon's residents will go their graves without ever calling the Sixth Line anything but the Sixth Line.

Despite the controversy, the sources of the names that now appear on Caledon's road signs are given here. They may not be popular, but at least they will be understood.

These brave women are early Inglewood bikers. Circa 1925.

Airport Road — This was, and still is, the road to the airport.

Albion Trail — This road recognizes Albion Township, one of the three townships that were amalgamated in 1974 and collectively became the Town of Caledon. The other two were Caledon Township and the northern part of Chinguacousy Township.

Ballinafad Road — This road is an extension of a road by the same name in the Region of Halton. It passes through the community of Ballinafad.

Beechgrove Sideroad — This name, selected by residents, honours an old schoolhouse.

Boston Mills Road — The road passes through the community of Boston Mills. Now only a cluster of houses, large cemetery and stone schoolhouse cum mortuary, it was once a booming town.

Bramalea Road — This is the extension of a road of the same name in Bramalea.

Castlederg Sideroad — Castlederg was the name of the post office in the area. It was named after Castlederg, County Tyrone, in Ireland, the birthplace of John Wallace. Wallace owned the local general store from 1852 until 1916. At some time between 1859 and 1877, the post office name of Mount Hurst was changed to Castlederg. Castlederg and Mount Hope were located on the Mount Hope Road, within a mile of each other.

Cataract Road — This road passes through the hamlet of Cataract. Its name was changed from Church's Falls to Cataract at the request of the post office. Cataract was chosen to recognize the local waterfall.

Centreville Creek Road — A creek by this name is a tributary to the Humber River. It runs through the hamlet of Albion that was formerly known as Centreville since it was roughly equidistant from the four borders of Albion Township.

Charleston Sideroad — Caledon Village was called Charleston between 1839 and 1853. It was changed at the request of the post office and became Caledon. Previously the village was called Raeburn's Corners after Robert Raeburn, who built the first house in the area in 1826.

Chinguacousy Road — This road goes by this name as it passes through the southern part of the Town of Caledon that used to be part of Chinguacousy Township. Chinguacousy is a native word that translates as small or little pines. Part of the Credit River once went by this name.

Coleraine Drive — In 1877, some one hundred people lived in Coleraine. This village was located just south of the Town of Caledon. The name is a contraction of the names Cole and Raine, two pioneer families who lived nearby. It was also called Frogtown, due to an abundance of frogs in the area.

Coolihans Sideroad — This road passes through the historic hamlet of Coolihan's Corners. This community was named after Mr. Coolihan, the owner of a popular hotel.

Creditview Road — This is the extension of a road that runs through the Region of Peel.

Dixie Road — This road is an extension of Dixie Road that runs through what was once a community by that name.

Duffys Lane — The Duffy family was one of the first families to settle in Albion and Eliza Duffy was an early methodist preacher. The original Duffy homestead near Bolton is a designated heritage site.

Mount Pleasant Road. Notice Toronto in the distance.

Escarpment Sideroad — This glorious road follows a route along the top of the Niagara Escarpment.

Finnerty Sideroad — The Finnertys were early homesteaders. Several Finnertys owned land along Finnerty Sideroad.

Forks of Credit Road — This scenic road passes by the forks of the Credit River. At this point the West Credit meets the Main Credit.

Glen Haffy Road — The Glen Haffy Conservation Area is in the same vicinity as this precious tree-canopied road.

The Gore Road — Toronto Gore Township was a wedge-shaped (gore-shaped) area east of Chinguacousy Township and south of Albion Township. The Gore Road passes through the old Toronto Gore Township.

The Grange Sideroad — The Grange was a community in the vicinity of Mississauga Road and the Grange Sideroad. It was so named because the agricultural society called the Grangers met there. It had a post office from 1876 until 1916, located in the McLaren Castle.

Hall's Lake Sideroad — A lake by this name is located on the Town of Caledon's easternmost boundary. It was named after George Hall and his family, who settled in the area in the 1830s.

Healy Road — This road is an extension of a road in Bolton.

The Forks of Credit Road is a driver's delight…even in 1945.

Heart Lake Road — Heart Lake is located just south of the Town of Caledon. It is surrounded by the conservation area of the same name. The lake, and therefore the road, derives its name from the shape of the lake.

Heritage Road — This is the extension of a road that runs through the Region of Peel.

Highpoint Sideroad — It runs along a high area on top of the Niagara Escarpment.

Highway 50 — This is a provincial highway and it was named by the province. There was discussion about calling it Queen Street, but it would have been expensive for businesses to change their addresses.

Horseshoe Hill Road — This is an extension of Dixie Road. Some people felt it was inappropriate to use the name of Brampton's roads in Caledon and petitioned for different names. This road passes by the site of the famous Horseshoe Curve of the Toronto Gore & Bruce Railway. In 1907 the train left the tracks at this point. Seven people were killed and 114 were injured in the crash.

Humber Station Road — The Canadian Pacific Railway once had a station near the Humber River at a site between Castlederg Sideroad and Old Church Road. The station closed but the name lives on.

Hunsden Road — This name recognizes an historical post office. Historical maps indicate that this post office moved a number of times but was always located in the area of what is now Hunsden Road.

Hurontario Street (Highway 10) — Also called Centre Line, Hurontario Street links Lake Huron to Lake Ontario.

Innis Lake Road — Innis Lake, a kettle lake, is found southeast of Caledon East. It was a popular tourist spot and is surrounded by land owned by the Innis family. The lake was once known as Scott's Lake in recognition of Isaac Scott, who built a mill on it in 1854. At one time, ice from the lake was sold to a company on Lake Simcoe.

Kennedy Road — The road is named after Thomas Kennedy. He was the Conservative MPP for Peel County for nine of ten consecutive governments. Twice he was the Minister of Agriculture. He was first elected in 1919 and retired at age eighty in 1958. This road continues right through Caledon since residents did not contest its application to what was the First Line East, Caledon.

King Street — This is an extension of King Street in Bolton.

Mayfield Road — This road passes through a community of the same name. Located at the Gore Road, it was once a bustling village with a brick schoolhouse, general store, blacksmith's shop and a hotel. A post office by this name opened in 1853. It was thought to be named after Mayfield, England. Nearby Mayfield Secondary School helps keep the name alive.

McLaren Road — This is an extension of Chinguacousy Road. Some people felt it was inappropriate to use the name of Brampton's roads in Caledon and petitioned for different names. The name is derived from the McLaren family that settled in the area. The McLaren Castle (on Creditview Road) was likely Caledon's most spectacular stone residence. Built in 1864 by Alexander McLaren, its nineteen rooms, turret and towers made it a landmark that was destroyed by fire in 1963.

McLaughlin Road — This road runs right into Brampton and is reportedly named after the developer by this name.

Mississauga Road — This road extends all the way to the City of Mississauga. It recognizes the native Mississauga, possibly descendants of the Ojibwa, who once occupied all the lands now included in the Region of Peel. The land was turned over to the government of Upper Canada in two deals, the final one in 1818. "Mississauga" means river with a large mouth and refers to the Credit River.

Mount Hope Road — A farm in the area just south of Old Church Road was called Mount Hope farm. It was owned by John Monkman. There were a number of Monkmans living in the area and a church nearby. Its post office was named Mount Hurst which later became Castlederg. However, the community of Castlederg was just south of Mount Hope.

Mount Pleasant Road — This road passes through a community by the same name. The Tremaine Map of 1859 shows a community on the Ridges called Mount Pleasant. *The Historical Atlas of 1877* indicates that the Mount Wolfe post office is located at the same spot. The Mount Pleasant Cemetery exists today.

Mount Wolfe Road — The Mount Wolfe area takes in land owned by the Wolfe family. The original Wolfe was John. He and his wife had thirteen children. They owned land on the Ridges, which is the highest point of the Albion Hills.

Mountainview Road — This is an extension of Torbram Road. Some people felt it was inappropriate to use the name of Brampton's roads in Caledon and petitioned for different names. By one account, it was someone's contention that Caledon Mountain could be seen from a point along this road.

Nunnville Road — There was a community just southeast of Bolton that went by this name. It was intended to be an early subdivision and was the brainchild of the Nunn family.

Old Church Road — This name commemorates the five churches that once stood along this road.

Old School Road — Some seven schoolhouses were once located on the stretch of road that bears this name. There are three left today.

Olde Base Line — The Base Line was the line that divided Chinguacousy Township from Caledon Township. After amalgamation in 1974, when there was no longer a dividing point between the two, the road became the "Olde" Base Line. Bert Moore credits the extra "e" to Clem Neiman.

Patterson Sideroad — This road was named after a family that settled in the area.

Porterfield Road — This road is named after a family of local settlers.

Puckering Lane — This road was named after a family that settled in the area.

Rockside Road — The Rockside Pioneers were some of the earliest homesteaders in Caledon. These Scottish settlers were duped by the Commissioner of Lands in York into taking deeds on property in the furthest reaches of surveyed land. The land is very rocky since outcroppings of dolostone rise to the surface in this vicinity. A community of Rockside grew up around these settlers.

Shaw's Creek Road — Shaw's Creek is a tributary to the Credit River. It runs from Caledon Lake through Alton. Its great flow of water was responsible for Alton's tremendous concentration of mills requiring water power. Duncan Shaw was an early pioneer who owned land in the area. He lent his name to this creek. Shaw's Creek is officially called the Credit River Alton Branch.

St. Andrew's Road — This road is an extension of Bramalea Road. Some people felt it was inappropriate to use the name of Brampton's roads in Caledon and petitioned for different names. This name is derived from St. Andrew's Presbyterian Church and cemetery that was built in 1853. The area was settled in the 1820s and 1830s by Scots from the Isle of Mull.

Torbram Road — This is the extension of a road of the same name in Brampton.

Willoughby Road — John Willoughby was an early settler with land on Willoughby Road just north of Highway 24.

Winston Churchill Boulevard — This road extends all the way through the Region of Peel. The source of the name needs no explanation.

CONCLUSION

This book makes much of man's accomplishments in Caledon. From the arrival of the first European settlers until today, humans have been taming the land, rivers and streams. Trees were cut, creeks dammed and houses built. Against great odds and despite considerable hardships, pioneers in the early 1800s scratched and scraped away in the forest until their harvest could supply more than their immediate needs. They uncovered limestone, hauling it out of the ground to be used for buildings at home and in distant places. They harnessed water to grind their grain, saw their logs, spin their wool and light their homes. They built magnificent churches, ambitious railways and efficient roads.

But in the name of progress, European settlers didn't always respect nature. In return, nature was often uncooperative. When too many trees were cut down, the soil blew away. When too many dams blocked a watercourse, salmon failed to return. When rivers were robbed of their forest cover, flow diminished and mills operated no more. Floods proved that nothing could be taken for granted, and fires were a constant threat.

When you look at a map of Caledon you see lines and sideroads, concessions and lots all aligned in a regular grid pattern. Almost without exception, pioneers followed these straight lines, building their houses and barns parallel to the roads and sideroads. When you come across a building erected at an angle as, for example, in the case of the Caledon Inn on Airport Road, you may be taken aback. You wonder what sets this particular building apart. Why is it out of order?

But as dominant as this grid pattern may be and as harsh as "progress" might have been, Caledon has maintained her character. What appear on maps to be straight roads have often been forced to wiggle and wind their way around bogs and forests, cliffs, hills and streams. An old schoolhouse may be a testament to the skill of stonemasons but without its backdrop of the Niagara Escarpment's cliffs it would be just another schoolhouse. If a century brick farmhouse weren't surrounded by one-hundred-year-old maples, it would simply be another building.

Without Caledon's rivers and streams, her flowers, wildlife, trees, vistas and nooks, this portion of the Earth would just be another place. But instead we have Caledon — and if we take care, if we have respect and allow her to flourish, if we learn to live with her so we don't have to tame her and she doesn't exhaust herself fighting back, our descendants will have Caledon too.

June 3, 1999

BIBLIOGRAPHY

A History of Peel County: To Mark Its Centenary as a Separate County, 1867–1967. The Corporation of the County of Peel, 1967.

Baillie, Susanne, Alanna May, Isabelle Schmelzer. *Bolton.* Erin, Ontario: The Boston Mills Press, 1989.

Beaumont, Ralph. *Cataract and the Forks of the Credit: A Pictoral History.* Erin, Ontario: The Boston Mills Press, 1973.

Beaumont, Ralph. *Alton: A Pictoral History.* Erin, Ontario: The Boston Mills Press, 1974.

Beaumont, Ralph, James Filby. *The Great Horseshoe Wreck.* Erin, Ontario: The Boston Mills Press, 1974.

Beaumont, Ralph. *Steam Trains to the Bruce.* Erin, Ontario: The Boston Mills Press, 1977.

Belfountain Village Church: 1835–1985 The first 150 years… Erin, Ontario: The Boston Mills Press, 1985.

Brown, Ron. *Ghost Railways of Ontario.* Broadview Press, 1994.

Bruce Trail Association, Trail Reference, Hamilton, Ontario: The Bruce Trail Association, 1997.

Cook, William E. *Cook's History of Inglewood.* Erin, Ontario: The Boston Mills Press, 1975.

Coombs, David G. *A History of the Caledon Mountain Trout Club.* Mississauga, Ontario: Speedy Printing Centres, 1989.

Cooper, Charles. *Rails to the Lakes: The Story of the Hamilton and Northwestern Railway.* Erin, Ontario: The Boston Mills Press, 1980.

Credit Valley Conservation Foundation. *Credit River Valley.* Erin, Ontario: The Boston Mills Press, 1992.

Crichton, Robert. *The Rockside Pioneers.* Erin, Ontario: The Boston Mills Press, 1977.

Dorin, Patrick C. *The Grand Trunk Western Railroad.* Seattle, Washington: Superior Publishing Company, 1977.

Filby, James. *Credit Valley Railway — The Third Giant.* Erin, Ontario: The Boston Mills Press, 1974.

Filby, James. *The Road to Boston Mills.* Erin, Ontario: The Boston Mills Press, 1976.

Heyes, Esther. *The Story of Albion.* Bolton, Ontario: The Bolton Enterprise, 1961.

Keough, Pat & Rosemarie. *The Niagara Escarpment, A Portfolio.* Ontario: A Stoddart/Nahanni Production, 1990.

Legacy: A Strategy for a Healthy Humber, The Report of the Humber Watershed Task Force. The Metropolitan Toronto and Region Conservation Authority, 1997.

Loyal She Remains, A Pictoral History of Ontario. Toronto, Ontario: The United Empire Loyalists' Association of Canada, 1984.

McKitrick, A. M. *Steam Trains Through Orangeville.* Erin, Ontario: The Boston Mills Press, 1976.

Mika, Nick & Helma. *Railways of Canada: A Pictoral History.* McGraw-Hill Ryerson Ltd., 1978.

Neufeld, D. "The Impact of Technological and Business Innovation on a Nineteenth Century Frontier: A Case Study in Central Ontario." Unpublished.

Pope, J. H. *Historical Atlas of the County of Peel.* Toronto, Ontario: Walker & Miles, 1877.

Ross, Oakland. *Caledon Ski Club: The First Forty Years.* Erin Ontario: The Boston Mills Press, 1997.

Roulston, Pauline J. *Place Names of Peel: Past & Present.* Erin, Ontario: The Boston Mills Press, 1978.

Stevens, G. R. *Canadian National Railways: Sixty Years of Trial and Error, Volume 1, 1836–1896.* Clarke, Irwin & Company Limited, 1960.

STORM Coalition. *Oak Ridges Moraine.* Erin, Ontario: The Boston Mills Press, 1997.

The McEnaneys from Cataract. Erin, Ontario: The Boston Mills Press, 1976.

Tovell, Walter, M. *Guide to the Geology of the Niagara Escarpment.* Ontario: The Niagara Escarpment Commission, 1992.

Trimble, Berniece. *Belfountain: Caves, Castles and Quarries in the Caledon Hills.* 1975.

Wilson, Donald M. *The Ontario and Quebec Railway.* Belleville, Ontario: Mika Publishing Company, Belleville, 1984.

Zatyko, Mary. *Terra Cotta: A Capsule History.* Erin, Ontario: The Boston Mills Press, 1979.

INDEX & PHOTO CREDITS

TOWNS, VILLAGES AND HAMLETS

Albion (the hamlet of)   35, 85, 110

Alton   18, 20, 29, 42, 61, 67, 68, 76, 106, 107, 108, 114

Belfountain   18, 20, 49, 52, 55, 65, 67, 89

Blackhorse   81

Bolton   9, 17, 20, 26, 29, 32, 33, 43, 71, 82, 88, 90, 92, 101, 104, 111, 112, 113, 114

Boston Mills   29, 34, 91, 92, 110

Brimstone   18, 48, 49, 52, 76

Caledon East   9, 17, 19, 26, 29, 35, 54, 55, 58, 60, 81, 82, 85, 88, 90, 98, 113

Caledon Village   24, 25, 29, 48, 55, 68, 93, 94, 107

Cardwell Junction   29, 33, 35, 82, 88

Castlederg   110, 114

Cataract   18, 29, 31, 36, 55, 57, 60, 61, 73, 74, 76, 77, 110

Cedar Mills   100

Cheltenham   18, 29, 34, 36, 54, 80, 82, 91, 97

Claude   29, 90

Ferndale   29

Forks of the Credit   17, 29, 31, 32, 36, 40, 41, 45, 47, 49, 50, 53, 55, 69, 74, 79

The Grange   49, 112

Inglewood   18, 29, 31, 34, 45, 49, 53, 55, 61, 69, 82, 91, 104, 105, 106, 107

Lockton   85

Mayfield   113

Melville   29, 32, 33

Mono Mills   29, 55, 80, 88, 89, 97

Mono Road   29

Palgrave   19, 20, 29, 35, 55, 70, 74, 81, 97

Rockside   52, 114

Rosehill   40

Sandhill   19, 87

Silvercreek   29, 39, 92

Sligo   69, 106

Snelgrove   23, 24

Terra Cotta   18, 29, 34, 36, 49, 53, 55, 70, 80, 82, 88, 90

Tullamore   88

Victoria   70

PHOTOGRAPHY

Jacket front (from top left, clockwise): G. Handley; courtesy of the Region of Peel Archives; G. Handley; G. Handley
Jacket back: G. Handley

Photos courtesy of the Region of Peel Archives: pages 10, 18 (upper left), 21, 24, 25, 29, 32, 33, 40, 41, 44 (bottom left), 49, 52, 60, 69 (bottom right), 72 (bottom right), 85, 101, 104, 105 (bottom right), 106, 109, 112

Page 31: photo courtesy of Buckstown Treasures, Palgrave
Page 53 (bottom left): photo courtesy of Art Von Zueben, Terra Cotta
Page 53 (top right): photo courtesy of the National Archives of Canada
Page 61: photo courtesy of Jim Dodds
Page 68: photo courtesy of Mary Lindsey Hunter
Page 69 (top left) photo courtesy of the Brass Thimble, Terra Cotta
Page 93: photo courtesy of Clayton Leigh, Hillsburgh

All other photographs: G. Handley